A Journey of Hope

Bob Parsons

An autobiography

AuthorHouse™ UK Ltd.
500 Avebury Boulevard
Central Milton Keynes, MK9 2BE
www.authorhouse.co.uk
Phone: 08001974150

Published by AuthorHouse October 2010
Previously self published in 2007
ISBN: 978-1-4520-7189-3 (sc)

This book is printed on acid-free paper.

Sex. Drugs. Violence. Rock and Roll. Not in this book! In fact the closest you'll get to any of these subjects is an occasional kiss, an aspirin, a few verbal fights, and a bit of ballroom dancing. Instead, you will find an honest look at my life, my thoughts, my feelings, and my continuing struggle to try and make the world a slightly better place.

If the book you are about to read appears to be egocentric in parts, I can only emphasise that I am uncomfortable using the "I-am-ness" term too often. But I cannot avoid it. I guess that is the nature of any autobiography.

Aye, Bob.

"An autobiography (must therefore) unless it is to become tedious, be extremely selective, discarding all the consequential incidents in one's life and concentrating upon those that have remained vivid in the memory."

'Going Solo'   **Roald Dahl 1986**

Acknowledgements

I would like to express my gratitude to the following, for their advice in putting this autobiographical account together - Gordon Wallace, Sally Prue, Jamie Wrench, Anne Smith, Simon Jackman, Tom Burke and Margaret Little. The main players who have made this all possible by their direct contributions are: Stuart Rees, Amanda Bate, Oliver Prentice, Jennifer Phillips, The Guild of Master Craftsmen, Pete Hardwick and my wife Ann Parsons.

My special vote of thanks goes to Julia Childs who patiently devoted many hours writing and rewriting the text in an interesting, expansive and humorous style. Without her, this book would not have been possible.

Finally, I want to thank my friends and the many, many interesting people I have met and been acquainted with along the road of life – through their writings – such as Robert Burns, Mahatma Ghandi and Aung San Suu Kyi, and through personal meetings with Mother Teresa and Nelson Mandela. I have also had the privilege of visiting sixty countries and learnt from their cultures and values.

This book is dedicated to my grandchildren Sarah Ming, Matthew and Charlie Becker and Jack, Joe and Finn Parsons.

All proceeds from this book will go towards the work of Hope for Children (HOPE), which I founded and registered in 1994.

Foreword

This inspiring story could be much longer, more reflective about Bob Parsons and his consistently supportive family, more savouring of numerous achievements in a crowded life. If there was more expose of the man, more superlatives about his courage and altruism, his inherent modesty would be rubbed away to reveal a larger than life character. Bob would not want that. So, even in this foreword, it's time to reveal his traits and applaud them.

There's a smorgasbord of experiences and adventures catalogued in a well-crafted book. Yet the chapters are often frustrating, though that comment is intended as an invitation to read between the lines and reflect on the mismatch between the values of Bob Parsons and the selfish and violent age in which he has lived. I'm going to use a touch of poet's licence and comment on the man I know as well as the book I've just read.

The trauma of an only child being evacuated three times from war torn London and then dispatched to an authoritarian English boarding school shows events which nurtured his courage and awareness of injustice. Spontaneous expressions of affection for his parents and deep appreciation of his father's working class loyalties became a main theme and a means of Bob re-charging his socialist ideology. His father's example was also the reminder of the principle of leaving the world a better place than when you entered it. This principle set the bar of life's challenges too high for most of us. Never for Bob. He has always wanted to jump higher.

The English probation service saw him as the friend and wise counsellor of hundreds whose offences were compounded if not caused by enormous social and financial difficulties. His compassion toward the people he supervised is legendary. He was the only person attending the funeral of a 71 year old man who had spent 57 years of his life in prison. In successive years he took groups of young delinquents to camp near the white cliffs of Dover. In the probation service, as in all his other initiatives for justice, Bob knew and lived the premise that social policy and practice should be about the dominance of altruism over egoism. His humanity was the standard of his professionalism.

As Director of *Save the Children* in Sri Lanka, Bob found the star role for which his playing in other theatres had prepared him. In a country engaged in civil war he travelled and built friendships, confronted riotous mobs and cared for thousands of vulnerable children. He encouraged and protected his staff. To Sinhalese and Tamils he stood out as a man to be loved and trusted.

The same leadership qualities appear in the creation of the international charity, *Hope for Children*. At a time when most men and women would have been hanging up their boots and calculating the size of their superannuation payments, Bob was responding to the cue given by Maisie, a Rwandan woman. Following her country's genocide, Maisie had given refuge to homeless orphans as large charities could not or would not immediately respond to her requests for assistance. Motivated by Maisie's pleas and given a timely bequest by a lonely ex prisoner whom he had befriended for years, Bob conceived the charity *Hope for Children*.

Aided by the indispensable stamina and support of his wife Ann, by his children and committed friends HOPE now provides substantial support to projects around the world. Bob still refuses to slow down or take a back seat. Despite bouts of ill health he travels to check the progress of projects and to give support to hard-pressed staff. In the months following the 2004 Boxing Day tsunami, I often tried to discover where he was. Seldom at home was the answer. More likely on the east coast of Sri Lanka inspecting projects concerned with basic needs for survival and with re-building homes.

In this work, as in his presence in several other parts of South East Asia, Africa and Europe, Bob paid little attention to his own needs. He knows how to be an international citizen. In the words of his numerous admirers, which means almost everyone who meets him, he has always walked the walk, never just talked the talk. The Queen awarded him the MBE and spoke face to face with him about his Sri Lankan years. But it's the approbation of the invisible and unknown citizens which Bob would value most: the ex- prisoners with nowhere to go, the amputees of civil wars who needed love as well as artificial limbs, the orphaned children whose parents might be traced, the poor families who needed food, medicine and furniture. At different times such people benefited from being on Bob's caseload.

He has already given much and has achieved what a full team of eleven or more players might not be able to equal. In cricketing terms he has scored many centuries, though he usually hit the boundaries in far away places on behalf of people who would not have the money to get into a ground or perhaps not even the strength to clap. Bob should appreciate this analogy. Despite his considerable skills and strengths as a rugby player, he was never much good at cricket. A snicked slice between second and third slip was usually his most exotic stroke.

For forty-five years I have been lucky to have had this man as one of my closest and dearest friends. He has always been courageous. He pays little regard for his own safety or well-being. He is highly principled but earthy, blunt, to the point. Neither egocentric nor self-righteous, his Quaker interests, his Scottish and working class origins and his irreverent humour ensure that dogma of any kind never appears on his agenda. He has wanted all the world's children to have hope and has been an influential advocate for vulnerable people of many countries and cultures. Never seeking reward for himself, or for Ann and other members of his family, he would not want his record written in neon lights. This foreword to the fascinating story of some of the key events in Bob Parsons' valuable life might embarrass him. But it's time that a large public knew of his generosity and skills, practiced always in the service of others. At last, this modest record of his life should give readers a chance to learn of a highly significant humanitarian and his far from modest achievements.

Stuart Rees
Sydney, July 2007

Dr Stuart Rees is Director of Peace Studies at Sydney University. He has had a very distinguished career in Social Work in the UK, Canada and Australia. He is a poet and author of many books including 'Passion for Peace'. He has just published his first novel ' The Prize'.

Contents

Introduction

I was in my fifties when my dad asked me the most important question of my life. It was a short, sharp sentence that I never will forget.

His profound words came at a time when he was on the last stages of his life. He had been admitted to St Georges Hospital in London with Alzheimer's. The illness had slowly changed him from a totally independent confident character, who at the age of 75 had still been rolling his own cigarettes, cooking stew, kippers, plums and custard and making home brew that he sold for seven pence a pint, into a needy, irrational and sometimes incoherent old man.

But on that particular autumn day, in the eighth decade of his life, dad became stronger than his illness, and the question I was about to hear was so powerful it almost knocked me off my chair.

"In your last moments of life, will you be able to say that the world has been a better place because of your presence?" he gently enquired, as he looked me in the eye.

I remained seated, my emotions rising, my lips almost paralysed, unable to reply at that moment in time.

But now, in the autumnal chapters of my own life, I am finally ready to answer my father.

1

The early years

Dad's parents

He wore a bowler hat. It rarely left his head. He kept his beloved bowler in place when he went to work, when he came home and even when he went to bed. He had fathered eleven children. Dad was the youngest.

My dad was working class and proud. He liked to bet on the horses, roll his own cigarettes, cook plums and custard, write short stories and walk the dog. Mum was convinced that he thought more of his blessed dog than he did of her. But it wasn't true. Dad had a heart bigger than the ocean. Most of it was devoted to mum and me, with a bit left over for the dog.

Chapter 1

I loved my father. I loved him in the same way he had his own dad – without hugs and emotion, but with an honest respect and understanding.

Dad was one of eleven. The baby of the family. He was born in May 1910, christened Maurice Alfred Parsons, but he was known as Jack. Together with his army of siblings he grew up in a four-bedroom semi in Colliers Wood, London, sharing a bed, an outside loo and a tin bath. It was a no frills, no nonsense, and no soft toilet-paper household. You did as you were told. Disobedience was not tolerated. Breaking the rules meant facing the punishing sting of the copper stick that was frequently used by his strict, disciplinarian mother. Even if you weren't to blame, you would still bear the brunt of that much-used weapon.

"That's for next time," she would warn as she delivered the strike, determined to keep her overpopulated household in order. But although her face was fiercer than an agitated Alsatian, her heart was warm and full of love for each and every one of her brood. And what a brood she had. Eleven mouths to feed. Eleven sets of clothes to wash with nothing more than a bar of carbolic soap, elbow grease, a mangle and the lethal copper stick. Eleven children to get out the door every morning and put to bed at night. Eleven lives to love and nurture in times of extreme poverty. And she even found room in her heart and home to bring up a twelfth child, her grandson 'Young Bill'. He was just a few years younger than dad and seemed to have inherited the gene of "cheekiness" that ran through the Parsons family. Dad and Young Bill were truly like brothers to each other. Whatever came their way, they stuck together and laughed together. Humour was a way of life for the Parsons family and a means of survival during hard times.

And times were harder than the bricks that dad placed on the coal fire each night and carefully carried upstairs to warm his bed. The country was struggling and so were the Parsons family. The First World War was claiming lives and wrecking lives. Unemployment was high and home comforts were low on the list of priorities. But dad knew life no other way. Like sardines in a can, he would sleep top to toe with his brothers in an over cramped bed, snuggling up to his brothers to beat the cold. "Sometimes we'd wake up to frost in the inside of our bedroom window," he had recalled. However harsh the weather, the Parsons brothers would have no choice but to wrap up warm and embark on a brief outdoor expedition to spend a penny each in the back yard outside loo. The call of nature frequently involved queuing in the cold, wind or rain. When it came to bath night, another long line would form for a weekly scrub in the tin tub. The bath water was recycled. It was full of softening soda and had already been used earlier in the day for the weekly Monday clothes washing ritual.

"We didn't go to school on Monday. Instead we helped ma with the washing. It was our job to keep the water hot and peg the clothes out to dry," dad had recalled. "We always got in trouble with school for being absent, but ma would say we deserved it."

Despite the harsh realities of his upbringing, dad was a fun loving, lean lad, who looked on the bright side of life. One of his favourite childhood antics was mimicking a local soldier who frequently practiced his sergeant major strut up and down his street.

"Left, right, left, right," the soldier repeatedly shouted, swinging his arms robotically. And as he marched with his chin held high and his chest puffed like a pigeon, the antics began. Behind him, falling in line, like a mini version of "Dads Army" was my father, his brothers and sisters and a small gathering of kids from the street. They meant no harm. But the war hero did not appreciate their innocent caper. Pulling the brakes on his well-polished boots, he would sharply "about turn"; chase them down the street and back to their own front doorstep. It was on that well scrubbed step that my grandmother came to their rescue.

Folding her arms across her chest, she would stand, as solid as a tank to defend her flock. Her fierce face would surely have made any grown man tremble. Taking on my grandmother would have been harder than fighting the Germans, that's for sure. She could have won the war with just one of her angry

Chapter 1

looks. The sergeant major always retreated and Grandma raised a faint victorious smile.

Grandad was placid in comparison. And shorter. To add crucial inches to his height he wore a bowler hat. Black. Neat. Symmetrically positioned. It was glued to his head day and night and even when he went to bed. As he climbed the stairs to bed at the end of the day, he not only took his hat, but a sword and whistle. "Just in case," he would state as he collected his weapons. In case of what? I shall never know. Perhaps, he used his sharpened sword to catch the occasional mouse that scratched round the skirting boards. Maybe he just wanted to be ready for intruders. Or maybe, just maybe he used that silver weapon to try and keep off my grandma's advances if she fancied an early night! With eleven children between them, he obviously didn't try too hard. It makes me smile to think of the old man, tucked up beneath the starched sheets, bowler in place, sword in one hand, whistle in the other, ready for anything the night may bring.

If I look at his photo, a precious, black and white snapshot, and if I search my memory, I can still see the twinkle in his eye. It was permanently there, shining like a star above his handsome handlebar moustache. He was the calming influence in the chaotic household. Rarely did his temper break, unless his precious sleep was disturbed. Then, all hell broke loose and the twinkle in his eye went out.

Dad remembers a night of commotion when his sister stole a late goodnight kiss with a boyfriend on the front porch below. Her romantic liaison woke the old man and throwing open the bedroom window above; he let his tongue loose waking the whole street. "I'll empty the chamber pot over you," he stated, cursing the startled couple below. The threat did little for their love life. They never smooched on their own doorstep again.

Raising a large family during the depression was a hard, uphill struggle for my grandparents. They used all the tricks in the book to make ends meet. Hand-me-downs and the well-muttered phrase "you'll grow into them" became a way of life.

Most of his recycled clothes did little for his street cred, but on one occasion, dad became the envy of the neighbourhood when a pair of nearly new cricket boots came his way. They were white as snow, barely worn and swiftly became the talk of the street. They turned him from a scruffy urchin into a top cricketer. The fact they were two sizes too big and slipped off his heel when he ran, just didn't matter.

Pulling them on with pride, he wore them everyday for school and every evening to play out in the street. I don't think they ever saw the fresh green grass of a cricket pitch but he walked tall in those boots.

My mother's upbringing was equally poor. She came from a family of three bonny Scottish sisters and a brother. The first-born was Helen (nicknamed Jock), then Mary (who remained Mary), followed by Elizabeth, who was called Betty, and then the baby of the family was William, known as Bill. Mum, who was christened Catherine, was known more affectionately over the years that followed as Kitty. She was the youngest of the girls.

In complete contrast to dad's upbringing on the war torn streets of London, mum lived in rural Spean Bridge near Fort William surrounded by striking skies, rolling hills and of course more than enough sheep to keep Scotland in woolly jumpers. Her childhood was as tough as the landscape. When, at the age of seven, her dad tragically died of pneumonia it became even harsher. He had been the breadwinner of the family. Without his wage, the family were plunged into deep financial crisis. Her mother was left with the responsibility of putting food on the table. Keeping her head high, she found a job, went out to work, and had little choice but to leave her children in the care of Jock, her eldest daughter.

Jock used the 'rod of iron' method to keep her siblings under control and get them fed, dressed and out of the house on the one mile walk to school. There was no bus service. No family car. Not even a bicycle. So every day, whatever the weather, and no matter how weary her young limbs, mum had no choice but to walk the two mile round trip to and from school. Kicking stones along the way, and running through the wind and rain until her long hair tangled and knotted, her young feet simply had to keep going.

Even the weekends gave her little time for leisure. Twice on a Sunday, pulling on her very best dress and polishing her second-hand shoes, she did the very same long route to the morning church service and then back again in the afternoon for Sunday school.

"I spent more time at church, than I did at home," mum joked. "I knew every hymn in the book. And every verse."

Mum (left) with her sister Betty.

By the time she reached her teens, her mother, Nin, had remarried. However, the new husband and stepbrother certainly did not bring joy into the household nor put a smile back on their mother's face. It was not a fairy story, happy ever after. Just the opposite. Mum had few kind words to say about her stepfather. Her brother William had such a strained relationship with the new man of the house that he was packed off to Canada to live with relatives. He was aged 14.

Soon after he had left home, the sisters moved to London to work. Mum decided to join them. She had just turned 15 and was far from worldly but she eagerly boarded the train heading south and waved farewell to the hills of Scotland.

"I was so nervous, but very excited," mum had recalled. "I'd never seen London before or even been on a train. I'd barely travelled beyond Inverness."

Mum (left) with members of her family.

Domestic jobs were plentiful in the city, and mum quickly secured a live-in position as a family cook. She was more than happy with her new job. She had work, a roof over her head,

Chapter 1

the run of a kitchen, good food to eat and a few shillings to send home at the end of the month.

So while my mother was settling into her daily domestic chores in Chelsea, dad was working in a fireworks factory on the other side of the Thames. He worked hard. All hours. He had no choice. A further education had been out of the question for dad and his siblings. Instead, they all learnt from the university of life.

Dad was forever hungry to discover more about the world and people around him. He found his own way to gain the knowledge he craved. At the end of a long day packing fireworks at the factory, he would spend endless hours visiting his local library. Pulling books from the shelves, he began a steady process of educating and politicising himself. Knowledge was a powerful tool for my father. It fuelled his opinions. It enabled him to confidently contribute to debates in the pub and over the dinner table. On one of his many excursions to the library he pulled a book from the shelf that later almost became a bible to dad. It was called The Ragged Trousered Philanthropists by Robert Tressell. Dad was inspired by the book. He wholeheartedly agreed with Tressell's proposal to 'build a co-operative commonwealth where the benefits and pleasures conferred by science and civilisation will be enjoyed equally by all.' Equality was ingrained in my dad's way of thinking. Following in his father's footsteps, it didn't take long for him to fly the red flag and become a firm labour party supporter. He lived by their strong socialist principles. He was red to the core.

At some point, when dad's head was not buried in politics, books, or stuck inside the fireworks factory, he set eyes on my mother. How their paths crossed I do not know. Where the first seeds of romance were planted is still a mystery to me. Somehow it does not matter. I can only guess that my mother's striking red hair, Mona Lisa type of smile, and strong natural looks, must have turned many heads including dad's. They were married in 1932 at Wandsworth registry office. It was a non-extravagant occasion, without a honeymoon, lavish presents or even a photographer to capture the occasion.

But the vows they exchanged were honest, true and lifelong. Side by side, 'for better or for worse, in sickness and in heath, for richer or poorer,' they were plunged into the harsh non-romantic realities of married life. If dad had carried mum over the threshold, she would have found herself entering a basic two-roomed flat where they struggled hard each week to raise the rent.

They had started a new chapter together, but just around the corner, two was soon going to become three. Just one year after my parents had tied the knot, my life began.

I was born in the early hours of April 12, 1933, a curly haired, much wanted, blue-eyed son. Home births were common at the time, but dad had anticipated problems with the labour. He was adamant that his first baby would be born in hospital. He was taking no chances and wanted the best for his wife and forthcoming baby. With cap in hand, dad made an unofficial visit to see the local Health Authority Official, eager to secure a hospital birth. Firmly, but politely, he made his request known. Firmly but politely, he was refused.

What followed next is an example of my dad's frequent efforts to stand up for your rights, be assertive and not accept second best. They were traits I would inherit from my father later in life. Leaning across the desk, and fixing a determined look on his face, he took the startled Official by the collar and made his request.

"A hospital birth. That's what I want. It's got to happen," he instructed. "See that it does. Got it?"

Dad got what he wanted for mother and baby. I made a safe entrance into the sterilised hospital room; screaming into life and making my parents swell with pride.

I was named Robert. A fine Scottish moniker. It was the name my father chose for me. Mum and her sisters had other ideas. They had wanted me to be called Angus and were seconds away from registering me under this name. Thankfully, dad put his foot down. Firmly. Solidly. Purposefully. He was good at that. "He's to be called Robert," he told the registrar.

I sometimes wonder when my parents held little Robert Parsons in their arms just what did they hope and dream for

Chapter 1

their son? Little did they know that ahead of me was a heart-warming, rewarding and wonderful life that would take me to the corners of the globe that dad had only read about at the local library.

2

Early Years

He was 10 years old. Twice my age. He lived with his mother in the top flat. We lived below. I was too young to know the term "special needs". But I did know this boy was "different". He could only watch through his wide eyes, unable to join in with the fun and games on the street. I was already becoming aware that all in life is not fair, that there is always an underdog, a weaker individual whose needs are greater than our own. It was a lesson that shaped my future.

The world I entered was a tough one. The country was struggling through a depression. Unemployment was high and like so many of our neighbours we were poor. Very poor.

My first home was basic rented accommodation in Wimbledon. A one-roomed flat without fancy comfy furniture or central heating to keep out the cold. We didn't even have a wireless. Dad was frequently out of work. His union interests and active involvement in labour party politics often went against him.

"Don't you worry Kitty, I'll get a job soon," he would confidently tell my mum. Bending down to kiss me in my cot he would leave the house in the morning and go in search of casual labour. Despite his hunger to roll up his sleeves and join the workforce, dad was denied employment time and time again. No work and not much play made Jack an angry but determined man.

Chapter 2

Me, aged one year and ten months

To make ends meet, we moved our few meagre possessions to a cheaper home. We didn't have the money for a removal vehicle. Instead, we used my big, bold, Silver Cross pram. Loading it up with clothes, plates, pots and pans and finally me, dad made several journeys backwards and forwards, pushing the pram the twenty-minute route to and from our new home and trying hard not to get the wheels stuck in the tram lines.

By the time I was five, we had moved a third time to a ground floor flat in Badminton Road, Balham. It was a busy well-populated area with a grocery on the corner. On one side of the street, was a row of spacious Victorian terraced houses, divided into small flats where families would share amenities and space. On the other side, 'the posh side', the wealthier folk inhabited one entire house themselves and a front garden. We lived opposite the posh. We didn't have a garden but a big bay fronted window where we would observe life on the other side of the street.

"They vote conservative, we vote labour," dad would boldly state neatly stamping his political views on the area. "And it's labour's policies that have enabled them to become posh!"

We shared our flat with my parents' friends – Dave and Catherine Cockburn. They were good folk who had a bright eyed, blonde haired daughter called Carol. She was a year younger than me, but a whole lot wiser. And prettier. Together, beneath the slate roof of our shared dwelling, we got along together in a practical, non-complaining way. Privacy was respected but our paths crossed daily in the communal kitchen or when we found ourselves outside the wooden door of the shared loo, nature calling us at the same time.

"You desperate?" I would ask Carol. "Are you?" she would reply.

Crossing my legs, I always let Carol go first, my urgent need for the toilet not as strong as my need to please her. She was like a sister substitute to me. I looked out for her in the street and she did the same for me. Her room, like mine was at the back of the house. It was small, dark, windowless space where I housed my collection of cigarette cards, my much-loved teddy and well-worn wooden building bricks. That was my lot. But I did not feel deprived. Nor did I suffer from living in such cramped conditions as outside my front door was an almighty, amazing, awesome and adventurous playground, or more commonly known as - the street. I had all the room in the world on that concrete space. The street was my jungle, a spacious car free zone where my imagination ran as wild as the children of the neighbourhood. It was the place where we all gathered to run, play, forge friendships, swap stories and give our parents a moment's peace.

We ran free for hours on end. Whatever the weather we would be out together, chasing, kicking or batting a ball. At that moment in time it felt like nothing in the world could stop our fun . . . nothing apart from the old lady who lived halfway

Chapter 2

down the street who we all called - 'Mrs Grumpy.' Mrs Grumpy certainly lived up to her name. She was grumpy by face and grumpy by nature and she liked nothing more than the chance to confiscate our ball if it accidentally strayed into her front garden. No amount of begging and pleading would make Mrs Grumpy hand it back. Several hearts would sink when she stopped our world.

As well as worrying about Mrs Grumpy, we had another concern. That was the fear that our much loved tennis ball may slip down the roadside drain. It happened occasionally. It was always a painful loss. Peering down the drain we would watch as our ball bobbed in the murky water, out of reach but not out of mind. It was the equivalent of losing an old friend. Every member of the street gang shared the grief. By the time we had lost a few balls in the same manner, I had, to my mates delight, devised an ingenious simple device to retrieve any treasures that fell into the murky waters below our feet. All it took was a little imagination, a tin can, a piece of string, a stick and a steady hand.

"Stand back," I'd say to my mates as I took control. Lowering the can down the drain I would carefully line it up so it dangled below the lost ball. Then, gently pulling on the looped string, I brought my catch back to dry land. Applause followed. I was a mini hero and my device was a winner. It was used time and time again to rescue any other stray balls spotted down the drains.

After scrubbing them clean, these extra supplies were sold on for a few coppers at a time and kept the street gang in sweets. I was a young entrepreneur and very proud of my invention.

At every opportunity I was on the streets looking for a slice of the action, or another tennis ball to fish and sell. By my side was my newfound friend Gordon Wallace, or Wally as he was known. He was tall, lean and well spoken. He lived opposite, behind the green front door, on the posh side of the road. Like me, Wally was an only child who was good at sport, even better at making me laugh, and a great help when it came to homework. "Copy mine," he'd suggest, if ever I could not complete my schoolwork. So I did. Frequently.

The Badminton Road street gang.
Wally is in the back row, centre. I'm carrying the flag!

Wally's dad worked hard for a national newspaper. My dad worked hard - looking for a job. But he continued to make his mark politically, taking his place in the anti-fascist marches that weaved through East London. Thousands would take to the streets in protest. Occasionally I accompanied him.

I knew nothing about the politics at the time but I sensed its great importance. Perched high on dad's shoulders was a glorious place to be. "Sit still lad," he'd instruct as I looked down on the crowd and the tapestry of trade union banners that were proudly carried along the way. I did as I was told, holding onto his head and tugging his hair, enjoying my grandstand view of London.

So my own little world and social circle was emerging. Apart from the occasional trips across London, my life centred around the street. The pavements and road were my playground. The nearby Oldridge Road School was my centre

Chapter 2

for fun, education and socialising. Wally was my best mate, Carol, the sister I never had, and living upstairs was a 'special needs ' boy who watched the world he could not fully enter.

I remember him well. Every morning, when I set off for school he would be perched on the steps beside our house his eyes wide open and a finger on his lip. Whimpering, he would look up and down the street searching helplessly and observing every movement that passed before him. His mother was worn down. Deep lines were etched across her forehead. She rarely smiled. There wasn't time in her life to stand still and take a breath. But somehow she coped with her lad's round the clock demands. I felt for him. I felt for his mother. She never got a break. And he never got the chance to join us at school, singing our hearts out in the morning assembly or running up and down the old wooden staircase to reach the classrooms on the third and fourth floors.

It would have been good to share school with him, just for one day. Yet, as much as I enjoyed my daily lessons, I could not wait for Saturday mornings to come round. This was the time of the week when I queued up outside the Odeon on Balham Hill for Saturday morning pictures. The queue was always long. And noisy. It snaked down the hill. Girls. Boys. Brothers. Sisters. Every youngster was eager and excitable. This was their weekly treat. Their only weekly treat. An hour or two of pleasure for a penny. But for those that couldn't rustle up the entrance fee, an emergency exit back door was left conveniently ajar. I never needed to sneak in, but many of my mates chanced their luck, slipping into the dark picture house like ghosts in the night.

Watching movies was the highlight of my week. Leaning back in the cherry red seats, swinging my legs while I sucked cheap gobstoppers, I was in my own seventh heaven. My spine would tingle as I observed the huge organ slowly and magnificently rising from beneath the stage. Twitching in my seat, I would take a deep breath and prepare myself to sing the Odeon's pre-film anthem. I can still remember the words that were always sung with gusto and joy.

'We come along on Saturday morning greeting everybody with a smile.' Everyone joined in. We all knew the words.

We all loved that moment. Then, at the end of the song, the organ would slowly disappear underground like a submarine plunging beneath the ocean. Giant draped curtains would slowly unfold and the movie flickered into life. Action films and daredevil antics on the big screen made my heart leap with joy. Any excitement I had witnessed in a film would be re-enacted on the street later that day, with Wally. I was the lone ranger one week, an Indian the next and Fred Astaire in between; it depended on the movie. It depended on the generosity of Wally's casting. Somehow he always got the best parts in the street remakes.

So as we played outdoors, with barely a care in the world, our country had a huge worry on its shoulders. The Second World War was about to begin. Constant news coverage on the wireless, and newspaper headlines were spilling over into our homes and hearts. I began to absorb my parents' concerns. They were worried. So worried that dad was rolling more than a few extra cigarettes over the course of a week. His roll-ups were part of the after dinner ritual. When the meal was over and plates were cleared, he would reach in his pocket, pull out his Golden Virginia tin of 'baccy' and snap open the lid ready for the rolling up ceremony. He could practically roll his ciggy's with his eyes closed.

I was fascinated by the effortless way he put together a much-needed fag and I seized the opportunity to lick the papers for dad before he completed his mission. Mum was also a smoker. She smoked like the movie stars, slowly puffing out wisps of smoke while I watched from the sidelines. Her weakness was Woodbines, long, thin, Woodbines that I often fetched for her from the corner shop in packets of five. Occasionally, when nobody was looking, I would put one of dad's cigarette butts in my mouth. I felt grown up just for a second but they tasted revolting. Watching the adults enjoy their daily habit, I would sit with them at the dinner table. Together, as they inhaled their daily dose of tobacco they also inhaled the latest news. Hitler and the Germans were coming, and life was soon going to dramatically change for every one of us.

Kitty and Dave Cockburn and Aunt Jock

3

The War Years

'Gott Sei Dank', (God is with us) read the bold engraving on my black leather belt. It was a gift from my father. He had posted it home to me just a few months after he left to join the army. I cherished that belt and wore it with pride during war games on the street. But the words of the engraving puzzled me. How on earth could God be with the Germans when he clearly had to be on our side?

I was at the tender age of six when my father walked out of the front door to take on Hitler and join the Grenadier Guards. He was going to Aldershot for a few weeks training. I did not know when I would see him again. I did not dare ask such questions.

I was proud of my dad. Proud he was going off to war. Proud he was going to play a part in fighting the enemy. Churchill had done a good job indoctrinating the minds of the young and old. But despite the propaganda, it was tough having to say "goodbye". I wanted to throw my arms around him and not let go. Standing on the doorstep, holding mums hand, I bit my stiff upper lip to hold back the tears. My mother, unable to keep a grip on her emotions, and failing on the lip biting technique, began to cry.

"Write to me," she called out to my dad a hint of desperation in her voice. Striding purposefully down the street in his too big boots, I watched him disappear from sight. Dad had a job

Chapter 3

to do for King and country. That's what Mr Churchill had told me. I also had a job to do, and that was to stay out of trouble, please my mum, and wait for the war to end. I was the man of the house now. Mum and me. Just the two of us. I would look after her... wouldn't I? In my short trousers and grey woollen socks I didn't look too convincing.

"Come on inside," mum said, taking my hand, shutting the door in an attempt to shut out her heartache. "Dad will be back soon enough." I fetched her the Woodbines.

"Course he will," I replied. We were both good liars but we didn't know it.

Almost every child in the street was fatherless. War had created a famine of men. All the male teachers had signed up, the shopkeepers too. Dads were as rare as bananas. Every corner you turned, the men had virtually disappeared and been replaced by women or a grandad variety of men. I missed the younger men of the neighbourhood. So did Wally. And no doubt my mum did too for very different reasons.

Wally's dad had joined the RAF. Carol's father had been enlisted in the Coldstream Guards. Like me, Wally longed for his father to come home, but together we faced the future together, side-by-side, the two young musketeers of Balham.

"Where's your dad gone?" I'd ask Wally. Shrugging his shoulders, he'd ask me the same question. We hadn't a clue which part of the world our fathers had disappeared to. We instantly missed them, and I questioned my mum endlessly about dad's return.

"When's dad coming home?" I'd enquire almost twice weekly. Patiently, mum would offer me the same reply: "He'll be back just as soon as he can Bob. As soon as he can."

I felt a mild desperation to see my father again. I wanted to be sure he was alright, yet, when he did unexpectedly arrive home on a 24 hour pass, I felt a distance between us that I had never known before. He seemed a different dad. More of a soldier than my father. I craved his attention but did not know how to approach this man in uniform. We shared time. But the clock was always ticking against us. I felt a great sorrow when the day was done and dad had to leave us all behind.

Dad on a 24 hour visit. Clapham Common, 1939

"Bye dad," I gulped, and I hugged him hard, wrapping my arms around his impressive uniform. Mum had a much longer embrace. I had no idea how much her heart must have been hurting. But she did her best to smile as he walked away, quickly returning to her war duties and her daily chores.

Mum, like almost every mother in the neighbourhood, contributed to the war effort by rolling up her sleeves and putting in many hours at the local ammunitions factory. Wally's mother pulled on a conductor's uniform and got a job on the buses. While our mother's worked hard we played hard in the street. Instead of tennis, chase and rounders, we all went to war on the pavements. Dividing our street gang into two, and arming ourselves with wooden sticks and pretend guns we staged endless fantasy fights between the German enemy and the British hero's.

That's when dad's belt got an airing. Wrapping it round my trousers twice instantly turned me into a nazi. And swapping my softly spoken London accent for a harsh Hitler voice,

Chapter 3

I selected my squad. It was an unspoken rule that the Germans would always lose. The belt meant I was always on the wrong side, but it didn't matter. The battle would be long and hard but a lot more enjoyable than the real versions we heard about on the wireless.

We staged our war in the deserted house at the end of the road. Nobody had lived there for years. It was damp. Cold. But it became our battlefield. Slipping through the ground floor window, we would position ourselves around the empty house, peeping out from behind dividing walls and open doors, firing imaginary bullets from wooden sticks. Our battles lasted for hours. Yet despite all the time I spent as a German, my foreign accent remained unconvincing. "Ya, ya, ya – nein, nein, nein," and a couple of goose steps was the best I could do to transform me into the menacing enemy.

At home, when the darkness of night fell over London and my belt was put to rest, I missed my dad. I longed for him to be sitting beside us at the dinner table, chatting about the day, and rolling his precious cigarettes. I longed for him to walk in the front door and fill the well-worn slippers he had left behind. I yearned for him to be back in the house, keeping us safe, keeping mum happy. I even yearned for him to give me a clip behind the ear. It was a difficult time of adjustment, but my relationship with my mum became stronger. Closer. Every night we would sit down together, listening hard for war news on the big brown wireless that sat on top of the mantelpiece. It was neatly positioned beside the long row of payment jars. They stood side by side like soldiers on parade. We had a jar for the electric bill, another for gas, and a third and fourth for rent and rates. They were stuffed with pennies and paper money that would frequently be dipped into for emergency use. Paying bills was a juggling of jars act. Mum was a great juggler. But more worrying than the prospect of paying the bills was the thought of dear dad fighting the Germans. Thankfully he had been spared being posted to Dunkirk. Instead he was bound for Africa. Young Bill was not so fortunate. The Germans had captured him just a few weeks after war started. How unlucky was that? I imagined him shut away in a small room, a POW fed on bread and water, while Germans patrolled the jail.

It was a worrying thought for a young lad of seven. So too were the nights we spent huddled together in the Morrison shelter in our home. The Morrison was huge. Stark. Ugly. It sat in the middle of the living room, its strong iron roof a makeshift table. I remember the day it arrived and the struggle to carry it into our home.

"Come and look at this, " I beckoned Wally. We examined the construction inch by inch. We tried it out. We climbed in. We climbed out again and repeated the drill several times.

As ugly as it was, we were glad to have a Morrison. When the sirens sounded, I would open the small side door ready for a long night in the cage. Mum, Carol and her mother were right behind me. Other families in the street would take their blankets and head for their own garden based Anderson shelters, or scurry to Clapham South or Balham underground stations. As the night stretched, and the night sky awaited the arrival of the enemy, we stayed safe beneath the protective iron roof, secretly praying for a peaceful night without bombs or without snoring. Huddled beside my mum, in my striped pyjamas. I felt relatively safe.

But life in London was becoming increasingly dangerous. Even more worrying than those nights in the cage was the alarming sound of the doodlebugs overhead.

I remember the fear. I remember my young mind anxiously waiting for that terrible sound to end, knowing that when it stopped, a huge explosion would follow. I hoped and prayed that our lives, and our house and Wally's would be spared in such moments. I didn't want the Germans to destroy my neighbourhood, my friends or my cigarette card collection and beloved teddy.

Food was always a comfort. Mum not only kept the 'home fire burning' but her oven burning too. She was a great cook, and served up the most memorable meals from what seemed to be just a dehydrated packet of onion, a bit of veg, an Oxo cube and bones. I can still recall the wonderful smell of her scotch broth bubbling away on the cooker in the corner of the kitchen. She boiled the butchers bones to perfection for that

Chapter 3

broth, and together we would sit, swallowing down her hearty vegetable concoction, wiping our plates clean with a big chunk of white crusty bread. It always made me feel better.

When times were tough, food, and mother love kept me going. We may have lived on war rations, but my dinner plate was always full and the love from my mother was plentiful. I never realised just how much that T.L.C. meant to me at the time. But in my adult years, when I visited orphaned children around the globe, it often came to mind.

Evacuation took me away from that mother love. It happened just a few months into the war; I had no choice but to leave mum's comforting scotch broth behind. My new home would be in Sussex. My temporary new guardians would be complete strangers. I was not happy about this.

"Do I have to go?" I asked. "Can't I stay here with you?" I pleaded.

Mum stroked my hair reassuringly. "You will be fine," she said. "It's an adventure, and I will come to visit as much as possible." I knew I had no choice in the matter. This was not an adventure that I wanted. The Germans and the war were annoying me now. The sooner my dad and Wally's father sorted them out, the better.

4

Evacuation

I wore a gas mask round my neck, a label on my coat, and carried a small holdall. Boarding the steam train in London, I pressed my face to the window, clutched my teddy close to my heart and waved goodbye to mum. I was totally unprepared for what was ahead. Rejection was a lesson I was soon going to learn.

"Can anyone give these boys a home? Could you please take in one of these children?" It was a simple request that my teacher repeatedly made as she knocked on the door of almost every house in the village.

We were in Copthorne in Sussex, a bunch of innocent young evacuees looking for a safe home. We looked a pitiful sight as we clustered together our young hearts heavy with worry. Behind us was London, our mothers, my German belt and Saturday morning cinema. Ahead was complete uncertainty. We had no choice but to put our total trust in the hands of the teachers. They knew nothing. Nobody did. There was no master plan made in advance, nor were any child protection issues observed. We were just stepping into a huge shambles in Sussex.

Robotically we followed a tired looking teacher down the street, hoping and praying that by the end of the day we would have a new home. The search for a safe refuge was a cruel process. One by one, without even looking back to say "cheerio" my classmates were offered a place to stay. One by one they disappeared behind various front doors. The young girls that

Chapter 4

looked to be trouble free were homed first, closely followed by the skinnier lads that would not be so costly on the food bill.

I was well built, taller than my peers, and had obviously had one or two of my mums scotch broths too many. Wally appeared similar. As our leaner classmates marched off into their new homes, Wally and I were left trailing our teacher, the only two boys without a place to stay. Being last on the list, hurt. It was a harsh selection procedure. My bottom lip quivered like jelly, my head was hung low, and my sorrow was obvious.

"Keep your chin up," Wally instructed, trying to introduce a bit of wartime spirit. "We'll be alright. You'll see."

He was right. As we dragged our feet down the street, we found our gold at the end of the rainbow. The treasure was a village store grocery shop. Knocking the door, our teacher once again boldly put her simple request forward.

"Can you offer these two children a home?" she asked, a hint of desperation in her voice. Wally nudged me.

"Smile," he whispered. And together, we did our very best double act big grin routine. We'd been practicing it all day. One nudge from Wally and my mouth would instinctively stretch wide open into what I hoped was a genuine smile.

It hadn't worked until now. But finally, the sight of my gnashers, and Wally's shining out beneath a Sussex sunset, succeeded in getting us a place to stay. After a bit of grown up whispering, the two elderly female shop owners agreed to take us in. My heart did somersaults of joy.

I was going to live in a shop. A shop that stocked everything including sweets. What's more, dear Wally was going to be with me. I glanced back at our new landladies – two white haired, frail looking spinster sisters. They seemed friendly. Old. But friendly.

"I'm Miss Viggers," said sister number one.

"And I'm Miss Viggers," said sister number two.

I was confused but tried not to show it. Shaking their outstretched boney hands, I was delighted I had found a home. A part of me just wanted to jump for joy; relieved that I did not have to walk the streets any longer. Instead I remained rooted to the spot, my mouth locked in a smile, until my teacher handed over our ration books and pushed us forward through the back door of the house, like two lost sheep being shunted into a pen.

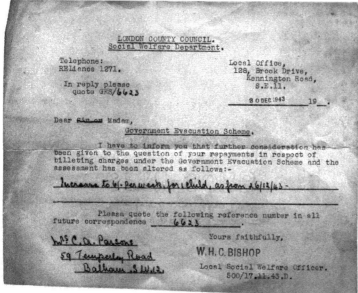

An evacuation paper

"Come along boys," said the eldest sister as she glanced us up, down and sideways. "There's a room upstairs you can share."

That night, in my new bed, I could not even fake half a smile. Placing my curly hair on the new strange pillow, I tried hard to settle. But in that small room, even with Wally close by, I felt that I was hundreds of miles away from the streets of Balham. I missed everything about home, especially my mum. It was an awful feeling. I did not dare share it with Wally. I wanted to be brave and adapt to my new surroundings. But most of all I wanted the war to end quickly so I could go back to London and dad could come home. If I had known then that war was going to last six years I would have cried all week. But in my young mind, where time is meaningless, I was certain that in a few weeks, Hitler the baddy would be defeated and everything would be the same again.

Chapter 4

"We'll be back in Balham by Christmas," I whispered to Wally several times from beneath the sheets, trying to convince myself that this strange new life would not be forever. "More like November," he casually yawned. Who were we kidding?

I adapted quickly to the routine as an evacuee. I had to. We were treated fairly and squarely and encouraged to be independent. Every morning while the sisters set up shop for the day we helped ourselves to a breakfast of toast . . . with jam if we were lucky. Life was okay for Wally and me. But some of my classmates were not so fortunate. The nervous bed-wetters were given a terrible time. Their tears were frequent and their young hearts pined desperately for home and the comforting arms of their mothers.

I got on with my new way of life and learnt to adapt. The sisters also tried hard to adjust. It couldn't have been easy for them to have their home invaded by two boisterous young lads. But I like to think that perhaps we brought a new dimension to their quiet lives and gave them the opportunity to do their bit for the war effort. They made us as welcome as possible but were equally relieved when we walked out the front door to attend the nearby school. Our lessons were in the afternoon. The local children took the morning shift. Segregation was not intentional. There was simply not enough room in the school for everyone. The system worked well and the days passed quickly. Breakfast. Homework. Chores. School. Tea. Bed. Same routine almost every day until those glorious occasions when mum came to visit.

Her presence and radiant glow put a smile on my face from morning till night. Hugging her hard we would step out together, mum impeccably dressed in a well cut stylish dress and neat heeled shoes and me running, skipping and jumping beside her in my long shorts and hand-me-down jumper. Holding her hand to make sure she stayed close, we'd spend the day together, strolling in the nearby countryside or taking a mini shopping trip to the nearby town. The thrill of mum taking me out to buy new socks, or walking through fields of green was absolutely memorable. I always hoped I could roll the day out, stretch it just a little longer so I did not have to say the inevitably tearful "goodbye".

Walking and talking we would catch up on the weeks that had passed. Mum always brought me news of dad and the street I left behind.

"Have we been bombed?" I'd always ask.

"No," she replied smiling reassuringly.

"Has dad written a letter?" was my other persistent question. Occasionally she'd snap open her handbag, take out an envelope and smile. She knew the content of those precious letters without even glancing at the page. She must have read them a million times or more. I loved hearing news from dad. His letters were brief. But the opening line was always a knockout.

"My Darling Kitty" mum would begin, and as she gently spoke those three important, loving words, her eyes would shine like stars in the night sky. Just three words were all it took to make my mum melt like ice-cream on a summers day.

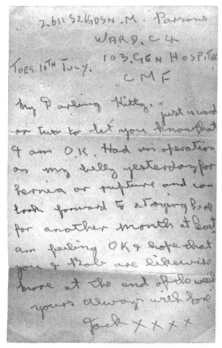

Dad's letter

Chapter 4

I often wished that dad would walk the streets of Sussex with mum on one arm and me on the other. It was a regular dream that I knew would not happen. Dad, I was told, was not allowed leave from his duty from the Eighth Army in Africa. I tried not to worry.

On one of mum's visits, she excitedly showed me a letter from her friend in Scotland. Opening up the envelope, she pulled out a thin piece of paper and unfolded it carefully. It was from her former school friend Maggie. Smiling at me, mum pointed her finger over the page.

"Read this," she instructed gently smiling. I did as I was told.

'You are always welcome to come and stay with us,' I recited as mum traced the words with her finger. Peering up at her for explanation, she smiled and calmly announced - "We are going to live in Dunoon Bob. You and me together." Dunoon could have been on the bloomin' moon for all I cared. What mattered was that I would be back with mum again. Squeezing her hand, I felt pleased with the news and hoped Wally would be okay without me.

So, just after I had arrived in Sussex I was packing my bag again, saying goodbye to Wally and the shopkeepers.

"I'm going to live in another country," I excitedly told him. "A place called Scotland." I didn't look back. Ahead of me, was a huge adventure. Hitler would surely never track me down in Scotland.

5

Dunoon Days

We ate fish for tea, breakfast and lunch. Fish so fresh it was almost moving on the dinner plate. And living in a small house by the sea, my love for Scotland began to grow. It was a love I would carry all my life.

The journey was long. Twelve laborious hours on a steam train from London to Glasgow followed by a brief blustery ferry journey from Gourock across the Clyde. The wind was strong, the water choppy. Mum placed a headscarf over her hair. I zipped up my jacket and felt the spray of the water on my face. My stomach churned on the waves. I'd never been to Scotland. I'd heard about haggis, the Loch Ness monster and the strong accents. I would soon see and hear it all for myself.

Mum and me were given a warm welcome in Dunoon. Maggie immediately called me the 'canny wee English boy' and introduced me to her children Jamie, Angus and Morag. I quickly settled into my new way of life, sharing a three bedroomed house that perched on the coastline just a stones throw from the sea.

It was a peaceful location where the only sound was the sea and the gulls . . . and Maggie's occasional ranting. She made sure I abided by the rules of the house. One of them was making sure we all said 'Grace' before each meal. Not the version I knew. But Robert Burns's Selkirk Grace which I swiftly learnt, accent and all, and remember to this day. Sitting round the table together, we would swiftly mumble the words,

Chapter 5

our minds concentrating more on the hot plate of food than on the meaning of the verse.

'Some hae meat an' canna eat
An' some wad eat that want it.
But we hae meat an' we can eat
An' sae the Lord be thankit.

No sooner had the last sentence been spoken than forks and knives would clatter on the plates as we plunged into our dinners.

Dunoon was different. Powerful. I spent many a moment just looking at the view from the upstairs window. Holding it in my mind. Capturing it like a Polaroid picture.

"What ye looking at?" Maggie would ask. "Is Hitler out there?"

Maggie and her children all had a raw, pure straight to the point, blunt Scottish way. They were unpredictable and never dull. The sea had the same characteristics. It was no ordinary sea and felt wilder than any other I had heard about before. I was drawn to the rugged coast line and would spend many an hour after school, watching the waves come in like thunder, crashing and whipping up a great froth while the gulls nose dived down into the water in search of supper.

Standing on the rugged landscape, my nose dribbling as I shivered against the harsh late summer weather, I discovered the true meaning of the cold. Powerful winds and relentless rain penetrated through my jacket and jumper. They had been sufficient for the mild English winters, but in Dunoon, I felt a cold that I had never experienced in my life. An hour or two in the great outdoors was more than enough to freeze my bones.

"Let's get the wee boy some extra clothes," Maggie stated when I returned from an afternoon in the wind and rain, my shoulders hunched, my teeth chattering and the drip from my nose almost forming a stalactite.

"Would you like that Robert?" she asked, stating the obvious. The severe weather had almost stuck my lips together. I could barely speak. Instead, I nodded my head top speed. Emergency supplies of extra layers were quickly found from the neighbourhood. They were not the best set of clothes I had seen in my life but I didn't care what I looked like, I just wanted to beat the cold. My new dark brown toggled duffle coat, gloves, and thick, hand knitted jumpers were greatly appreciated. I wore them all at once, adding inches to my size. But I felt as insulated as a thermos flask of hot tea. Snugly wrapped, my time outdoors increased.

Years later, the memory of being frozen to the bone on Scottish shores came back to me. At the time, I was taking caseloads of clothes to an orphanage for disabled children in Bulgaria. The weather was alarmingly extreme. Sub-zero temperatures that could wipe out the weak, the sick and the unprepared, were common. In the orphanage, there was no cosy double-glazing or central heating. Windows were broken, conditions were harsh. Children shivered. But within minutes of my cases being handed over, the clothes were swiftly distributed and gratefully pulled on to beat the cold. Smiles erupted. Just a few cases of clothes had made such a huge difference to these orphans. In Dunoon, just a handful of garments had the same smile inducing result on me. Additional garments meant I could face the wind and rain without the pain of frozen bones. Consequently, I spent hours on the shoreline. It was a perfect place for me to run, meet friends and lose all track of time. While the weather raged, I turned over rocks, prodded at crabs and bounced stones on the sea. Occasionally, I thought about Wally and Sussex and the shop and the bed-wetters I had left behind. I felt lucky in comparison.

Trying to understand the harsh local dialect was more of a challenge. I really was in a foreign country. The language baffled me. And so did the well-used Scottish sayings that I did not understand.

"It's a braw bricht moonlicht nicht the nicht," Maggie would often state as she looked out the front window.

"Yes," I would politely answer. "I mean no," I would add, hoping my reply was appropriate.

On other occasions when Angus and Jamie spat their words out faster than a crashing spitfire, I would shrug my shoulders, and mutter, "pardon", forcing them to slowly and

Chapter 5

painfully repeat their sentence, breaking it down into English, until I grasped the meaning. They were a fun trio. The youngest lad Jamie was a mischievous, bold comedian.

"I'm the class dunce, I always get to stand in the corner at school, " he boasted on several occasions.

"Oh?" I replied, unsure what to say.

"But I'm not just any dunce," he quickly explained. "I'm the head dunce." He seemed almost proud of his witty title. We all need to be good at something, I thought to myself.

Maggie, and her other two offspring, were equally fun loving and demure. I grew used to their upfront, sharp humoured blunt ways of dealing with life. They did not mince their words nor take things to heart. School was the same. Teachers were far stricter and far more direct with their instructions than those I had experienced in London and Sussex.

I began to toughen up a little as I adapted to the ways of the North. The soft edges of my character were sharpened and my gentle manner moulded into a slightly hardier way of being. I became more frugal. More confident. A new me was evolving.

I was in no rush to leave Dunoon behind. I had settled well. But my brief stay in Scotland was soon going to be over as quickly as it had begun. Just as I was beginning to grasp the local dialect and make new friends Mum announced we were moving. We were heading to the South West to Port Isaac in Cornwall to live with her sister Mary and her three daughters Thelma, Jean and Catherine who had moved out of London.

I didn't want to go. Once again, I had little choice. Waving goodbye to Maggie at the station I left Scotland behind beneath a cloud of steam. Another chapter would soon be coming my way. But my three months stay in Scotland had left a deep impression. My love for Scotland had been born; my Scottish roots had begun to grow, watered undoubtedly, by my brief time in Dunoon, and to this day, I love to return North of the Border and find the time and space to switch off. Iona is a favourite retreat. Supporting the Scottish rugby side through thick and thin is also a favourite pastime. And I need little excuse to wear my much-loved Clan MacDonald tartan kilt.

6

Port Isaac

The telegram was bleak. My uncle had been severely injured in service. He would be discharged immediately. Tears fell as my aunt and mum inhaled the bad news. Comfort came in the form of lard. A lump of white fat was left on the doorstep wrapped in oiled paper. It was a gift from the locals. They wanted to show their compassion and support. Lard was as rare as nylons and oranges. We now had more than enough to go round. I hated the Germans for injuring uncle Charlie, but I was glad we had lard.

I will never forget that lump of lard. I will never forget the reason it was left on the doorstep of my aunt's quaint old Fisherman's Cottage in Port Isaac, nor will I forget the emotions that unfolded that day. I'd been living in Port Isaac for seven months when a knock on the door stopped our world for a few moments.

"There's a telegram for you at the post office," said the young lad on the doorstep. Awkwardly, he looked to the ground. I looked at mum. She looked at Aunt Mary. And Aunt Mary looked up to God. She was gasping with shock. She knew that a telegram could spell out death or injury of a loved one.

It was bad news. Very bad. I remember the tears that flooded the living room when they returned from the post office, telegram in hand. I remember my aunt and mum clutching each other sharing the pain while I kicked the rug and walked round the edge of the room waiting for an explanation. Mum finally broke the news.

Chapter 6

"Your uncle has been badly injured," she explained, anger and emotion rising in her voice. "Its his leg. They've damaged his leg. It's a terrible injury. Terrible."

For a few moments I stood there my mouth wide open, the harsh reality of war hitting me in the stomach. My mind went into overdrive. My imagination ran wild as I visualised him legless and limping across the battlefield to save his own life.

"Poor Uncle Charlie," I thought. He'd gone off to war a fit, healthy young man, a great athlete, a father of three girls. He had a whole future ahead of him. But now he was going to be coming home with just one leg? How would he walk? How would he get around? How would his life be with just one leg?

I hated the Germans for hurting my uncle. I tried not to think too hard about the detail of his injury but all sorts of disturbing images ran through my mind. I dreamt up numerous scenes of how he must have fallen following an explosion. I pictured him sat up in his hospital bed. I created graphic scenes that were more powerful than the movies I had watched at Saturday morning cinema in Balham.

Just a few hours after the telegram had arrived the lard was delivered on my aunts scrubbed stone doorstep. It had been left there as a goodwill gesture, a supportive symbolic offering to show my aunt that the people of the village were thinking about her and her family.

Mum seemed surprised by their gift. Me too. The locals had never been over friendly towards the 'English evacuees'. They made sure we knew we were the outsiders. They just kept their distance, smiling politely from afar.

But on this tragic day, the day of the telegram, all barriers were dropped and the hand of friendship was offered. It was deeply appreciated and gave us something to talk about for the rest of the day. I tried hard to focus on something positive and not to think about my uncle's plight.

Apart from the telegram, life in Cornwall ran smoothly and predictably. Every second month, we would be joined by mum's oldest sister Jock who worked in London for the Ministry of Food, as a dietician. Jock was responsible for advising how meagre war rations could be best used to provide all vitamins and nutrients needed in a daily diet. She was a great source of nutritional knowledge. She knew the vitamin, fat and fibre content of almost everything edible. Jock was an intelligent lady with a college education. She had also fought in the International Brigade against Franco and the fascists in Spain. Jock enjoyed her time in Port Isaac, and the chance to catch up with family. She made a fuss of me. I liked the attention and was content with my new surroundings. But as much as I enjoyed living in the all female household, like so many lads my age, I constantly craved male company to substitute my missing dad. That was the main ingredient lacking in my life.

Mum by the sea at Port Isaac

Fortunately, I found what I needed in a local teenager called Jack. He worked for the local butchers. Every Saturday morning, come rain or shine, I helped him take meat deliveries around the area. We started at 4am. Our form of transport was horse and cart. It was like a scene from an old fashioned movie. Man, boy and horse plodding through the cobbled west country streets while the sun rose over Port Isaac splashing its rays over the rooftops, warming up the morning.

Chapter 6

Those moments we shared were precious. Jack would be holding the reins and I would be holding onto my joy and excitement. Jack seemed like a big brother to me. I couldn't get enough of him and looked forward to our Saturdays together meandering through the narrow lanes and bumpy tracks, the cart loaded with meat. When Christmas came, an extra delivery of a bumper sized chicken was made at my auntie's house.

"Look at the size of this bird," my auntie gasped as I placed the sumo wrestler sized chicken in her hands. "There's enough meat here for the whole street." Our bellies were more than full that year thanks to my connections with the local butcher.

Sitting round the festive dinner table, the meat spilling over my plate, I thought of dad. I wanted him home. I wanted him to be part of this gathering. As I tucked into my Christmas pud, I silently prayed he would be home soon, and if God couldn't answer that prayer I asked him to help me find one of the silver threepences hidden in my dessert. I was doubly disappointed.

But instead of dad I at least had Jack. I wanted our morning delivery round together to be part of my life forever. War deprived me of this pleasure. One chilly spring morning, just as we had nearly finished our work, Jack gently broke the news to me that he would soon be leaving the West Country.

"I've got my papers," he said. "I've been called up."

His words hit me like a punch in the stomach. I remember tears raining down from my eyes as I realised he would soon be gone. I felt rejected. Devastated. Distraught. The cobbled streets of Port Isaac suddenly did not seem so appealing. I wept into my pillow that night, angry with Jack and more than angry that this stupid war was taking him away from me.

Jack's departure from Port Isaac soon became gossip on the streets. The locals were not happy that he had gone against Cornish tradition and joined the RAF instead of the Navy. They turned their back on him completely.

"Is the Navy not good enough for him?" they commented.

"Who does he think he is?" they stated.

I didn't care whether Jack joined the Navy, RAF, the Army or the Salvation Army. What mattered to me was that he was not going to be a part of my life any more. I was thoroughly frustrated with war and the way it seemed to stretch on forever and mess up your life. The only warming thought amongst the gloom was the good news that Uncle Charlie's leg was going to be okay. Miraculously surgeons had sewn him back together again and patched up his injury. Amputation wasn't necessary. He'd never run a marathon, but he'd at least be able to limp some of the way.

Uncle Charlie must have been one of the happiest men in the West Country when he saw the streets of Port Isaac and his family again. He celebrated his homecoming with a drink, a good meal and plenty of loving from the woman he left behind. His son Colin was born nine months later. It was meant to be.

7

Boarding School

The food was terrible. The prefects were even worse. We lived on a daily diet of bland powdered mash, regular lashings, public humiliation and sport. Like it or lump it, this was the life as a boarder at Wilson's Grammar School.

"Don't scrape your feet. Don't drop paper. Don't fail at sport. Don't look up when you should be looking down. Don't cry. Don't laugh. Don't complain. Don't get homesick. Don't answer back. Don't sneeze, cough, fart or burp. And don't ask for more."

Had I stepped into a scene from Dickens' Oliver Twist? It certainly felt that way. There were so many rules at Wilson's Grammar School. Too many. It was a tough regime. Break the rules and you knew about it. Corporal punishment was common. The prefects had been handed over this ridiculous responsibility and frequently over abused their authority. Six strokes was the average punishment for a mild offence. And what felt like fifty for more serious matters. It was part of the regime. The skin on my backside grew thicker. It had to. It was almost impossible to be a good lad all the time. After the freedom of Port Isaac, I initially hated almost every minute of my life as a boarder.

I hadn't wanted to leave the West Country and go through yet another goodbye ceremony. But after a year in Cornwall, dad had sent word from Africa that he wanted me to get the best education possible. Wilson's Grammar, which had moved from London to the outskirts of Horsham, was the priority.

Unfortunately, I passed the interview process and gained a place as their youngest recruit. I could not complain. It was what dad wanted. He thought he was doing the right thing for me. But in my young mind, it was completely the wrong thing. The only consolation was that Wally would be attending the same school. Our paths would cross again. I couldn't wait to see my old mate Wally, but I was in no rush to start at Wilson's.

"It's what your father wants," mum had explained.

"It's not what I want," I protested. I had no choice. I kicked the skirting board, tutted loudly and rolled my eyes to the ceiling.

From day one I detested being a boarder. I didn't want to spend night after night in a hostile dormitory, tucked up in the bottom bunk of a squeaky steel framed bed. I didn't want to live in fear of being picked on by prefects, humiliated by other boarders, bullied by teachers. I didn't want to feel the sting of a six-stroke punishment that was dished out morning, noon and night for absolutely no reason. I didn't want my precious stamp collection to be stolen from under my pillow or to have to answer to the nickname 'Parsnip'. I wanted to be back in Balham, dad home, mum making broth, and my mates knocking on my door to play out in the street.

The teaching staff were well past their sell by date. They were a weary, white haired bunch that had been called out of retirement to return to the classroom. They made no secret of their reluctance to work again. Wherever possible they delegated their workload.

Morning assembly started the day. It was a stiff, ceremonial occasion. Shoulder to shoulder we stood up straight. We replied, "Yes sir," when the head asked a question. We sung a hymn or two a day, repeated the school motto 'to be, rather than to be seen' and prayed hard. "Dear God, please get me out of here," was my usual request. But the Lord was far too busy to help me, so every morning I'd be back in the school hall ready for the daily gathering of boarders.

Singing hymns was a light relief to the tedium and rigid discipline. I always sung my heart out. 'Jerusalem' was my favourite. It touched parts of me that other hymns did not reach. I felt a sense of patriotic pride when I joined in with the words.

Chapter 7

The school pianist must have been equally touched, as he would bash out the notes with firm precision, building up the volume and jerking his head in rhythm. By the time we got to the second verse, I was singing so hard I almost forgot how much I hated being a boarder. It was a brief escape. Once the assembly was over, the reality of the daily regime became clear again. I had to find a way to survive. And within weeks, I learnt that if you can't beat a system you have to join it. The best and only way to get along at this bloomin' boarding school was to be a winner. Sport and coming first were the name of the game.

My secret plan was to turn myself into an Olympic athlete, a top footie player and a cricket legend all rolled into one. I was going to achieve this by the end of the term. I'd show these "beastly" boys what I was made of... wouldn't I?

So I joined the football team; I put my name down for cricket and cross-country. I lost weight on the meagre rations, and as the weeks rolled into months, I stopped coming last and started to show real signs of improvement. This pleased the prefects no end. Even more pleasing was the day I became the hero of the chess team. It all happened at an inter school under-fourteens chess challenge against the upper class, fee paying Christs Hospital School. The battle was staged in the school hall and my game was the last of the afternoon. By then the whole team was peering over my shoulders willing me to do well. You could cut the tension in the air with a knife. If I won, or drew the game, we scooped the tournament. If we lost, my life was as good as over. The pressure was on. Concentrating hard, I pushed pawns, I moved my knight, I took deep breaths, I let my opponent sweat while my heart beat faster than a steam train going downhill with the brakes off.

But after a few cunning moves, a touch of psychological pressure, a bit of luck and a quick prayer to save my soul, the moment of glory was nearly mine. Smiling confidently, I looked my opponent in the eye, slowly pushed my queen across the board and sighed. I had wrapped up the match. We had won by just half a point. I was a hero, a winner, a top boy, and the crème de la crème of the chess team. And what's more, my reputation would soar.

Behind me came a loud cheer and enough back patting to nearly push me over. "Well done Parsnip," the prefects muttered. "Excellent stuff." Rising to my feet, I glanced at the row of ecstatic young lads smiling back at me. Today I was a somebody at Wilson's Grammar. I was more than pleased with myself.

School life improved after the chess challenge. I had learnt the useful skills of being able to adapt and survive. Others were not so fortunate. Many boys were desperate for some tender loving care. In search of affection they would fake an ailment or illness and join the long queue to see the school matron. She knew there was little wrong with most of these lads but she was the only substitute mother for miles. And the only female in an all male environment. A sticky plaster, a bandage, or a tablet administered by matron worked wonders for many a boarder.

Morale was also lifted when mums came to visit. Waiting impatiently at the school gates, my stomach would do cartwheels when I caught sight of mum arriving. Throwing my arms around her, we would go for a stroll in the nearby lanes. Sometimes, we passed the American soldiers who were stationed near the school awaiting the invasion of France. They had the reputation of having too much chewing gum and money. I was always pleased to see them strolling by and would smile politely while mum blushed gently by my side.

That evening in the dormitory I would relive every footstep I had walked with mum. But my thoughts went out to the boys who did not have visits or letters from family. Their heartache was obvious. However hard they tried to hide their tears, it was impossible. Not even a sticky plaster moment with matron could ease their pain.

And just when boarding school seemed like it would go on forever and a day, the news we had all been hoping and praying for was announced one morning in assembly.

"Boys of Wilson's Grammar. I have some very important news for you," the Head said as he stood before the school, trying hard to contain his joy. And clearing his throat and holding his chin high he smiled triumphantly.

"The war has ended," he announced, almost shouting. "We have won the war. Germany and their allies have been defeated.

The school will be moving back to London in the near future. But now let us celebrate this great moment."

His sentence was barely finished when two hundred jubilant boys began to cheer, clap and jump for joy. Their euphoria filled the room, bursting out the windows and almost raising the roof. Grabbing Wally, we hugged each other hard, and thought of our dads.

We had a week of celebration at school. Union Jacks were draped around the school, Winston Churchill speeches were played on the wireless, flags were waved, 'Jerusalem' was sung with even more gusto and school meal portions were doubled. It seemed like a permanent smile was on the face of every single boarder and teacher. Nobody needed a plaster that week. Matron had the quietest time she had ever known. Winning the war meant dad would soon be home, and we would all be together again back in Balham. I couldn't wait.

At Wilson's

8

Back Home

He was a stranger to me. I hadn't seen him for five years. I called him dad. He called me son. But we didn't know each other anymore.

Dad didn't talk much about the war. Some of his mates never came home, a few of them returned with shell shock and a mind full of nightmares, others just wanted to ease back into their old life and not look back.

But I wanted to know everything about dad's wartime adventures. I was more than keen to find out where he'd travelled, how many bombs had rained down on him, and how he dodged the Germans. Determinedly, I pressed him for information. When he ignored my requests for knowledge I became even more annoyingly inquisitive. But dad kept his war experiences close to his heart. He shared only one story. It was a tantalising tale about a journey he made through Northern Africa to Italy. It was a story well worth the wait. Sitting down for dinner one evening he shared the experience. Slowly.

"I saw Arabs passing by on camels," he began as he chewed his food and paused for breath.

"Wow," I replied, delighted that dad was ready to talk.

"They were real Arabs with cloths wrapped round their head to keep off the sun and sand," he continued.

"Wow!" I repeated and dad smiled remembering the moment.

"You know what son?" he added, his eyebrows knitted together as he leaned towards me.

"What?" I replied, the excitement running through my veins.

Chapter 8

"One of those Arabs winked at me. He just sat back on this camel and winked," dad added, demonstrating the wink with his right eye.

"Really?" I added, totally immersed in his tale.

"Yeah, and when I looked closer, when I looked at the face beneath the cloth, I noticed that the man winking wasn't an Arab at all. You know who he was son?"

Dad paused before the punch line and began rolling a ciggy. He knew how to spin out a story. My patience was pushed to the limits. I held my breath, desperate to know what happened next. Dad lit his fag and continued.

"Who was he dad? Who was he?" I enquired, my mind bursting to know the whole story. Between puffs of tobacco, dad completed the tale. "That cheeky winking camel jockey was one of my mates. He'd gone AWOL son. Absence without leave. He'd broken the rules and taken off with the Arabs."

Dad fell over laughing as he reminisced on his pal's great escape across the desert. I sighed and let my imagination run free as I pictured the fake Arab friend trying to ride all the way back to Blighty by camel. Mum giggled and dad gave her a loving look. For a brief moment I felt jealous.

As much as I wanted my dear dad back home, I felt pushed out just a little. Mum was no longer mine alone. I had to share her now, compete for her attention. The real man of the house had returned.

I didn't really know my father anymore. He'd left when I was seven and now I was almost a teenager. My voice was on the verge of breaking. My hormones were kicking. I was not the little boy he'd left behind. I'd missed him terribly over the years of war but it was going to take time for our relationship to grow.

Mum wasn't having the same problem. There was more laughter in the house than ever before. She wore a permanent smile. So did he.

We all settled back into London life together and did our very best to compromise and adjust to each other. Home was at 59 Temperley Road, Balham and there was a new addition to the family . . . a small, brown haired mongrel dog called Shebe.

Mum and dad after his demob, 1945

Dad had bought Shebe for fifteen shillings at Petticoat Lane market, a good buy as far as he was concerned but Mum wasn't too happy when he walked her into the living room.

"Meet Shebe," dad had grinned. "She needed a home."

"You'll both be needing a home if she doesn't behave" mum quickly replied.

But Shebe had impeccable manners. She was also a great guard dog and a fantastic bed warmer. To my delight Shebe always slept at the foot of my bed, curling her canine limbs carefully into position over the hot brick that was placed beneath the sheets. Shebe was not good at sharing. She refused to budge and make room for my long legs. But I didn't mind the slightly cramped conditions. I was never cold with Shebe around.

Shebe was a legend in our house. Dad liked nothing more than to take her for long walks across the nearby Clapham common. They'd come home sodden, muddy and ready to collapse in front of the fire.

"Give her a bath son," dad would instruct, if Shebe came home particularly grubby.

Having a bath was a big occasion at home. A ritual that took time and effort. First, the tin bath tub would be placed in front

Chapter 8

of the fire. Then, mum would fill it up with every available saucepan full of boiled water. Finally, when the tub was ready, I would strip off in the back room, jump in the bath and scrub my skin till it was almost sore. And while the fire blazed, I became squeaky clean.

After soaking myself, Shebe would be led into the water. (If dad had his way, Shebe would have been first in the bath). Shebe hated the humiliation of standing knee deep in my grime. To retaliate she would make sure she showered us all with one of her grand fur shaking stunts. Nobody escaped a small soaking. One small shake and the water would spray everywhere. Hastily, mum would run round with a towel mopping it up. I still have the old tin bath from those bygone days but it's never been used since.

The alternative to sitting in the tub at home was a trip to the local public baths. I'd use this system of cleanliness whenever I got covered in mud playing football. Twenty baths sat in a long row and 20 bathers sat inside them. Luckily for Shebe, dogs were not allowed.

In this public centre for cleansing, the water was centrally controlled. So if you fancied a long soak and the water went cold you would simply call out "hot water for number 5." Getting clean at home was preferable to seeing all shapes and sizes scrubbing away their daily dirt, moaning when their hot bath dropped a few degrees.

"What's happened to you?" dad would ask when I arrived home from the public baths, my curly locks, sprung like coils and still damp.

"You look different. What's that smell?" Then he'd sniff my hair and smile. "Been to the baths?" he'd ask. "I didn't recognize you looking so clean."

Dad seemed happier than I had ever remembered him. In the months that followed the war he had decided to set up in business with Young Bill and his brothers Walter and Reg. Putting their heads, skills and demob money together, they became 'Parsons Builders'. Mum was their secretary. I was their spare time helper. It was a winning combination. They were in demand.

Parsons Builders, Tooting, 1946

At weekends, I would lend a hand. It was my job to push the loaded wooden handcart down the road to the next job. That cart had a mind of its own and took all my muscle power to get the wheels rolling.

When I wasn't sweating behind the cart, I learnt all the tricks of the trade from my uncles. They taught me how to mix cement, bang in nails, lay bricks, and knock down walls. But most of all, they taught me one of the important lessons of being a man on a building site . . . and that's how to swear! Words I had never heard before and words I never dared even think would fly around the building site with the London pigeons. In their hardy work boots, the Parsons brothers' language was dirtier than a sewer. In their slippers, back at home, sitting down for dinner at the end of a long day, their words were almost as soft and sweet as sugared marshmallow.

Like all kids, I was keen to copy the adults and have a go at swearing. I just had to give myself permission and hope I didn't get in trouble.

"F-ing hell, I'm soaked," I cursed one afternoon as I stood by dad's side picking up rubble in the pouring rain. Dad glanced

Chapter 8

sideways at me and raised his eyebrows. I'd been longing to say that word for weeks. It felt fantastic.

"Bloody f-ing blimey," I tried the next day and smiled with satisfaction.

"Its just my bloody sodding luck," I added hours later for my grand finale swearing encore.

Dad tried to swallow a laugh and made me promise never to use such language in front of mum, Shebe or at school. I never did. School was certainly not the place to swear. I was still attending the strict, disciplined Wilson's Grammar. It had been relocated to Camberwell in South East London. Same school. Same rules. Different location. I was relieved I was not a boarder anymore. But instead of falling out of bed in my dormitory I faced a long journey across South London on two buses. It was touch and go trying to get to school on time. Frequently I failed. No excuse was acceptable. Missing the morning deadline meant joining any other latecomers for a heavy caution from a red faced angry head teacher. One pupil who accompanied me for a morning caution was a cheeky faced young lad by the name of Caine. Michael Caine, the Oscar winning Michael Caine who went on to appear in more movies than I can remember. He lived near school. I can't pretend we were great mates. But we did meet in the mornings for a caution or two. I'm not sure what his excuse was for being late but my reason was work related. I had an early morning paper round. Before I'd even had my breakfast, I was running round the streets, delivering my heavy load and taking a sneaky peep at copies of Beano, Dandy and Wizard comics that were also on their way to various letterboxes in the neighbourhood. The paper bag was always heavy. And the dogs that barked behind front doors were irritating.

To keep my spirits high and give me one-upmanship on the menacing barkers, I would take great delight in rolling up a paper and firing it like a torpedo through the letterbox. My target was of course the snarling, four legged menaces. My paper torpedoes silenced a few dogs in the neighbourhood and I always felt victorious at every hit placed on target. I felt sure my canine capers could have been featured each week in the Beano.

After the paper round, I'd dash home; grab a few slices of toast, pull on my uniform and run like the wind to the bus stop. Then I could relax just a little. Dressed in my black blazer, cap and tie, I would perch on the open topped deck of the number 35, feeling like I was king of the castle. Larking

One of my better school reports

around with my mates we would watch the world go by below. On a good weather day, it was a joy to be there. On a bad weather day it was an endurance test. You either faced the rain, cold, sleet, wind and a soaked school uniform or joined the rest of the travellers crammed downstairs. I didn't fancy pneumonia, so always opted for a crushing below.

School was as tolerable as the bottom deck. I was not a natural academic but I wanted to please my parents. My relationship with dad had strengthened since his post war homecoming. We were mates. I did not need to compete for mum's attention anymore there was room in her life and heart for the both of us.

Sometimes, on a Sunday, I accompanied dad to the local pub – The Grove. It was a handy five-minute stagger away and belonged to a bookmaker. Pubs at the time were strictly male terrain. The women stayed home. And while their husbands downed pints, I knocked back a soft drink and watched the games of 'pitch and toss' unfolding outside.

To take part all you needed was a few pennies, and a good pal who could keep an eye out for the police. This was hardly hardcore gambling, but it did not go down well with the local Bobby on the beat.

If the heavy boots of a curious copper came close, a shout or whistle went up and the gamblers would clear all evidence of their illegal game in the blink of an eyelid. I never joined in with pitch and toss. But I loved to be a spectator. It would always be an entertaining afternoon watching the locals throw a coin against the wall hoping it landed nearest to the marker so they could scoop the winnings. Mum would complain if we were late home for Sunday dinner.

"Your roast's gone cold," she'd moan, putting it back in the oven to warm it up again. Hot, cold or lukewarm her Sunday dinners were memorable.

Aside from pitch and toss, dad enjoyed an occasional gamble. Horses and greyhounds were his specialist subject. Ever since his late teens he'd studied form, known how to "run books" and occasionally had a sixth sense on which nag would win the race. He'd once scooped 25/- in a race. A shilling bet was all it took, the horse came in at 25 –1 and he just could not believe his luck.

"The bookie even told me to take my shilling elsewhere next time," he recalled.

Dad still liked to put the occasional few bob on the greyhounds and would spend an occasional evening at the track in Wimbledon with my Uncle Charlie. If his timing and judgement were accurate, he'd arrive home on the bus, a couple of pints later to show off his winnings. If he lost it all, he'd walk the 2.5-mile route back, his pockets empty, his head hung low cursing the canine for not running fast enough.

"That damn dog was half asleep," he'd complain. "Waste of space her being on the track. She'd be better off on the butchers rack."

The other great passion in dad's life was football. Wimbledon and Chelsea were his teams. When he had a few bob to spare, and even when he didn't I'd accompany dad on a trip to Plough Lane to watch Wimbledon play 'the beautiful game'. Our mode of transport was dad's 'James' auto bike. It was a boneshaker of a machine with a 98cc engine and a toolbox on the back. I sat on the toolbox. And without helmets or a care in the world we'd chug through the streets of London together. It was hardly the most comfortable of rides, but I would have sat on dad's shoulders if it had meant I could go and watch a game of soccer. I loved football and those crisp autumn afternoons when we'd stand on the grass sloped terraces shouting for our team. Everyone wore caps. Everyone huddled together in wind and rain. There was never any trouble and if Wimbledon won, dad's auto would fly all the way back to Balham. We'd talk about the game over dinner, reliving the goals and the joy. Mum wasn't bothered about football and didn't know her offside from her backside, the cross bar from a bar of chocolate, but she was happy to hear our post match gossip.

After a season or two at Wimbledon, dad took me to Stamford Bridge to watch Chelsea. They were in the first division. In comparison to Wimbledon's amateur footie that was played in the Isthmian League, they really were a dream team. As soon as the turnstile creaked and I entered

Chapter 8

the 'shed' end of the ground, my young heart would soar with anticipated excitement.

Pushing our way through the block of supporters we would try to find a good viewing location. My height was against me. It was not easy at four foot something to see the pitch.

"Can you see here?" dad would ask, as we moved left, right and sideways.

"No," I would reply time and time again.

If luck came my way I would be lifted off the ground, above the crowd and carefully passed down over rows of heads until I reached an obstruction free position at the front.

With dad behind me several bodies back, I let rip and sung, shouted, screamed and cheered with the solid block supporters.

"Come on The Blues," I'd scream till my throat was sore. And for ninety minutes, I'd roar for Chelsea, knowing dad was somewhere behind me, singing the same songs, shouting the same names of our football heroes. We were close at those matches. Even closer if Chelsea got the result they needed.

I have so many Chelsea moments, etched in my memory. But one match in particular stood out from the rest. It was in 1951/52, the last home game of the season and a crucial day for team, and supporters. We were playing Bolton. What's more we were playing to survive. If Chelsea lost, drew or did not score at least three goals we would be relegated to division two. Tickets for the match had sold out. But dad didn't give up trying to get into the match. With me following in his footsteps he circled the ground asking friends, strangers, and street sellers, if they had two spare tickets for the game.

"If there were crocodiles in the Fulham Road and Chelsea were at home to Biggleswade, the fans would still cross the crocodiles to get in," remarked one of the street vendors, Joe Smith, who had been supporting Chelsea since the day he was born. "It's sold out mate. Can't help you."

So, instead of the terraces, Dad and I joined a huge gathering of supporters who stood shoulder to shoulder on the pavements of Fulham Road, just outside the ground. This was in the days before pub television. Instead of watching the coverage on a television screen, our ears, like radar, tuned into the sound of the crowd. We knew what the score was just by the roar.

"Goal," we all screamed when the crowd erupted in the stadium. Chelsea were 2-0 up when fifteen minutes before the final whistle, dad decided to take advantage of a gate that had been opened to disperse the crowd.

"Follow me," dad instructed. With barely time to take my hands out my pockets, we scurried into the ground, pushed our way onto the Shed end of the ground and smiled victoriously at each other. That final quarter of an hour of the match was a glorious bonus. We watched the Blues score two more goals. They had survived relegation by a goal average of 0.044. It was a miracle moment.

Dad threw his cap in the air. I leapt up and down clapping loudly and longing to be a famous footballer. The match had fuelled my yearning to be a soccer legend. Like every boy that stood on the terraces that day, I wanted to run down the wing, the crowd shouting my name. I longed to bang in goals and punch my fist in the air. I wanted to be just like my favourite players, Tommy Lawton and Roy Bentley. That's all I wanted.

Jimmy Hill was my other football hero. He played for Fulham but had started perfecting his on-pitch skills as a teenage lad, playing for the Boys Brigade. In my imagination, just like Jimmy, I would one day play for a top team. In real life the story was not so sweet. I played slightly above average soccer for the Boys Brigade. We trained weekly on Clapham common, and I tried to put into practice the skills I had witnessed at Stamford Bridge. I was a good enough player but not good enough for a position in the Chelsea squad. I tried hard. Whatever the weather I was keen to turn up every week. Changing rooms were non-existent. Instead we would all get changed in the comfort of the nearest hedgerow, and throw our clothes into a carrier bag.

After the match, I'd return to the hedgerow or nearest bush and peel off my muddy clothes. Every lad did the same. We'd be dotted round the common, hopping from one leg to another as we tried to hide our flesh from any passers-by.

On one of those moments, I got the shock of my life. To my

Chapter 8

absolute horror, I stumbled over an abandoned dead baby wrapped in a blanket, tucked inside a hedge. The sight of a new life turned to stone by death, almost stopped my heart momentarily. I ran for help, my legs almost buckling. There was nothing that could be done for the baby. But I felt a cocktail of fear and sorrow. It was my first encounter with death. My grave discovery became the gossip of the week amongst my mates.

The Boys Brigade had become a big part of my life. Three times a week I'd look forward to their meetings at the Ramsden Road church hall near my home. And on the Sabbath, I would pull on my Sunday best and join their bible class. The Boys Brigade was a disciplined, character building environment that firmly encouraged sport, socialising, camping and caring but firmly discouraged girls. 'Steer clear from the opposite sex' was the moral message taught by the two ageing Wooderson brothers who ran the 88th London Company.

'Don't date girls yet, you are far too young,' we were repeatedly told.

They meant it. One of my pals was sent home from the annual camp on the Isle of Wight for breaching the rules. I think he was guilty of holding a girl's hand and making her a cup of tea with sugar. She was obviously sweet enough. He paid the price.

The Wooderson brothers made sure they practiced what they preached. Both of them were confirmed bachelors. And only when one of them died later in life, did the younger brother breach the rules and get married at the age of 65. I'm sure he made up for lost time and maybe even rewrote the Boys Brigade anti-female policy after his wedding day.

Girls, as far as I was concerned were a fascinating but very different species. I watched them from afar, keeping one step back. I was far too shy to move closer. They had the habit of making me feel awkward, self conscious and stuck for words. Apart from growing up with Carol in my early years, and spending short periods of time with my Cornish female cousins and with Morag in Scotland, I had little experience in socialising with the opposite sex. I did not know how to talk to them, what to say, and what not to say. I pretended I wasn't bothered, but deep down inside, I was itching to break the Boys Brigade rules and step out with a girl on my arm. Sadly, the only stepping out I did was with Shebe on her regular walks round Clapham common.

How I longed to be like my good friend Paul Turner who I met at the Boys Brigade. He attracted girls like bees to the honey pot and seemed to have more girlfriends than I'd had hot dinners . . .which judging by my healthy childhood waistline was quite a few. He had the looks, the charm, the physique, and the girls. I was envious.

Dad sometimes teased me. "She was winking at you son," he'd grin when we walked past a good-looking girl in the street. "Ask her home for tea. Go on son. Go on."

Gently blushing, I'd quicken my pace. I was annoyed at dad for embarrassing me, but more annoyed at myself for feeling so awkward in the presence of young women. If I could have wished for any one thing at that stage in my life, it would have been for a lorry load of confidence with the opposite sex. I wanted that even more than I wanted to play for Chelsea.

By the time I left school at the age of 16, girls were constantly on my mind but not in my diary. The world of work distracted me. I was about to start a job as a trainee manager with a printing company. Dad said it was a great opportunity and would expose me to all aspects of the industry. I would attend evening classes at the North West London Polytechnic, studying for a City & Guilds Full Technological Certificate in Typography, and more importantly, I would bring home £2 per week. Mum seemed pleased with my job prospects and delighted that I would be able to make regular contributions to the Parsons housekeeping pot. It was always half empty. Or half full according to mum's mood.

Dad was now working at the GPO offices. Parsons Builders had folded following a disagreement between the brothers. He seemed happy enough with his job and even happier I had stepped onto the first rung of the career ladder.

"This will be a good trade for you son," he'd urged. "One that will last a lifetime." I nodded my head automatically. My

Chapter 8

own thoughts on work and life beyond Balham, had not been shaped yet. I did as I was told. The wider world, and hopefully women, would come my way later.

9

Working Life

I was worn down and worn out. Work was exhausting. Studying was a hard slog. And I still hadn't found a girlfriend.

The company was called Wightman's. They were fair and square, like many of their workers. But, as long as I showed willing, they would give me all the skills I needed to become a trainee manager in the print industry. My future was sorted. My working life had begun. Routine. Predictable. Unsatisfactory. At 7.00am, after tucking into a plate of porridge, I caught the underground train from South to North London. It was almost as crammed as the lower deck of the number 35 bus that I had boarded for school. Part of me wished I was still making that journey. Work in comparison was serious, grown up stuff and I was not quite ready for this inevitable chapter in life.

"Morning," I would beam as I stepped into Wightman's offices, a fake smile on my face.

"Morning Bob," came a chorus of replies. And my day unrolled. Same time, same place, similar routine. And two quid in my pocket at the end of the week. I made the tea, ran errands, swept up on the print room floor, worked alongside compositors and did as I was told.

In the months that followed, one of the skills I acquired was how to rip off the customer without them realising. "Always add 10% when you are pricing up," I was instructed. "Then, tell the customer you are going to give them a 10% discount."

Chapter 9

"Okay," I replied obediently, my eyebrows rising at the company policy. It didn't sound right at all, but I kept my thoughts to myself. At that time in my life I was just content to be part of the workforce and keen to learn and do well.

By the end of the day I was often exhausted. Summoning up reserve supplies of energy I would travel to Camden Town three times weekly to study at North West London Polytechnic. The weekly schedule was punishing and far harder than my time at Wilson's Grammar. But I kept going. My parents had instilled in me a work ethic and the importance of finishing what you start. That theory also applied to dinner.

Even though war was firmly behind us all and ration books were a thing of the past, we always cleared our plates until they were squeaky clean. Every single scrap from the bones was also devoured.

Meal times were painful for Shebe. She was constantly disappointed. Her well-rehearsed wide-eyed "gimme gimme" look was wasted on our family.

With work demanding so much of my time, I had few opportunities to socialise. But I had made progress with the girls. Well, just a little, although I still lacked confidence and always tended to undersell myself. I had started a dance class. Nothing fancy or foreign. Just plain and simple ballroom dancing. The waltz and the quickstep were the first steps to master. To learn this fancy footwork meant finding a partner. Preferably a girl.

As much as I liked my mates, I was not keen to put my arms round their waists and lead them through a slow waltz. So instead of holding back and risking being the only male without a girl, I disposed of my awkward shyness and held out my hand to anyone who looked female.

One or two of the girls only just qualified. They were hardly the prettiest things on two legs. But I would dance with them all. I wasn't fussy. I couldn't afford to be. As the saying goes – a choosey man is a lonely man.

Clasped awkwardly together with my chosen partner, we clod hopped our way round the dance floor. I lacked grace. I lacked star quality. I was not born to dance.

"One, two, three," I would count, concentrating hard on the music, my feet, and the feel of a girl's waist.

Some of the girls - the more rounded variety, didn't have waists. Others had sweaty hands or the occasional wart, and one or two of the more popular females kept their distance. But a few of my dancing partners were as light and beautiful as ballerinas. They reminded me of the Fred Astaire and Ginger Rogers movies I'd watched with Wally at Saturday morning pictures. My feet somehow always let me down when I danced with those top movers. I couldn't glide across the floor like a swan. My style was more of a John Wayne stagger.

"I suggest you learn to walk before you learn to dance," scowled the female dance teacher. The class laughed. For one moment I wanted to run out the door and never return. Instead I let my mouth smile and I laughed loudly. At myself. It was a winning strategy. I quickly learnt that if you didn't take yourself too seriously, it was the way to a girl's heart.... well at least the way to get yourself another dance. Girls liked to giggle. If I couldn't win them over dancing or with dashing looks I could at least make them laugh. Hopefully with me, and not just at me.

Socialising at the dance classes slightly boosted my confidence with the opposite sex. At work, I had finally turned one female head in the office. Her name was Veronica. She was tall, dark and hands on! And quite a few years older than me.

"She'll tear you apart," the lads at work joked. I couldn't wait. We shared a few great moments together – talking, walking, and having a bite to eat. It was nothing serious, but it was a start.

Dad was keen to meet Veronica. "Bring her round for a cuppa," he encouraged. I made excuses. Deep down inside, I didn't want Veronica to see that I came from a home that had an outside loo and poor inside conditions. I was ashamed. Embarrassed. I wanted to impress my girl, not send her running. Mum wasn't so keen to meet my first girlfriend. She blatantly discouraged the relationship progressing any further.

"She's far too old for you," she commented. "Far too old." I didn't care. Turning at least one head was good for my morale

Chapter 9

and for a brief moment in time, until Veronica exchanged me for another eager young love-hungry suitor, I had no problem getting to work early.

10

Conscription

I wore a blue battledress uniform and an RAF beret. I learnt how to march, salute, stand at ease and obey orders. But most of all I learnt how to bite back against the bullies. There were plenty of them in national service. I despised them all.

If there was one period in my life that I could say was an almost complete waste of time, it was the two years I spent in national service. Doing your duty for the country was, of course, compulsory. There were no "ifs," "buts" or "maybes." Unless you had terrible eyesight, flat feet or no feet you had to leave your home, job, loved ones behind and become an unwilling conscript.

I questioned what I was doing. I had become interested in the Quaker way of life, which supports pacifism and is opposed to the concept of settling issues by force. I was tempted to register as a conscientious objector. Instead, I followed the pack. Reluctantly.

But from the moment I pulled on my uniform and walked into Padgate Camp at the age of 18, I knew that this was not the life for me. The eight-week basic training was harsh. Tough. Ridiculous.

Corporals with nothing much to do, took great delight in picking on the new recruits and making their life a misery. They reminded me of the prefects at Wilson's Grammar School. Not a pleasant memory.

We were all given a number. A bunch of numerals became

my identity. I was not Bob Parsons any more but 2531484. I will never forget that number. Never. It was drummed into me night and day by the corporal bullyboys.

"2531484 Parsons ," I would shout out when I lined up to receive my meagre weekly wages of 28 shillings minus any barrack room damages. (A shattered light-bulb meant reduced wages to just 24 shilllings if the bulb happened to be dangling above your bunk).

"2531484 Parsons," I would repeat, when we were paraded or inspected. In the decades that have followed I have forgotten crucial phone numbers, dates, and birthdays. My conscription number, I will recall when I am ten feet under!

Mentally, there was very little stimulation in national service. I took up smoking. A fag or ten a day beat the boredom. There's only so many times in one week that you can clean your boots, run round a field or do a series of press ups. The corporals simply ran out of tedious tasks for us to do. Smoking gave me a moment of bliss in a long day of tedium. With every puff, I remembered dad and his roll ups, mum and her Woodbines. A cigarette helped me knuckle down and reminisce.

Discipline was a national service priority. Free thinking was unacceptable. The name of the game was to obey. I soon became a top contestant. If they had asked me to hop up and down on one leg singing the national anthem I would have done so.

One lad in particular was having a harder time than most. His name was Stanley. He had a low IQ and was struggling physically and mentally with national service. He should have been exempt. Every hour was a struggle for him. He could not keep up with the regime and sunk lower every day. It was painful to witness. Sadly, wherever there is weakness, bullies surface. It didn't take long for the corporals to make mincemeat out of him. He quickly became their daily target for abuse. No matter how hard this innocent victim tried to co-operate, he was hounded, hassled and humiliated. He went to bed each night a broken man.

"You're a bastard, what are you," the vicious corporal would tell poor Stanley as he stood inches from his face, eyeballing him with a look of disgust.

"I'm a bastard," he would obediently reply, time and time again.

Stanley was near breaking point. I felt his pain. I absorbed his sorrow. One afternoon, when the bullies were once again picking on their prey, verbally kicking him when he was down, and smiling smug smiles of satisfaction at their antics, I decided I could stand it no longer. My blood was boiling. My mind worked overtime. I remembered Robert Burns wise words:

'Firmness is enduring and exertion is a character I always wish to possess. I have always despised the whining yelp of complaint and coward by resolve.'

So I decided to exert myself and open my mouth. Loudly. "Leave him alone," I snapped at the corporal.

Twenty or more of my colleagues, turned their heads, barely able to believe my outburst.

"Leave him alone," I repeated, speaking out as if my life depended on it. Spinning round on his heavily polished boots, the corporal marched towards me. Left, right, left, right. Fire. I was on the receiving end of a verbal hurricane. Anger and venom poured from his mouth as he promptly gave me a piece of his mind. I seem to remember it was quite a big piece. I wanted to tell him he looked uglier than a gargoyle. I wanted to tell him I did not have a hearing problem. But I let him rant on loudly. It was what he did best. I didn't care. I would remain standing after his oral attack. I could take it. But what I couldn't take had been watching my poor pal suffer a minute longer. He was the underdog. The runt of the litter. He needed help, not bullying.

My punishment came in the form of potatoes! I was put on "jankers" and ordered to peel a sack load of spuds in the kitchen. One by one, I skinned those spuds until my fingers were sore. Just when I thought my mission was complete the corporal smiled smugly and pointed me in the direction of an aircraft hanger. Inside was a mountain of potatoes. Hundreds of sacks were stacked up ready for peeling. "There you go Parsons," the Corporal smirked. "Open your mouth again and you can peel this lot." Peeling spuds was just one of the many

Chapter 10

pointless and humiliating punishments dreamt up by the Corporals. Digging the garden with a dining fork or painting coal white was also on offer.

Over the years that followed, I have made a habit of speaking up for the underdog, even if it does mean swimming against the tide. Perhaps I have been influenced by Harper Lee's book *'To Kill a Mockingbird'* in which one of the main characters in the book-Atticus advises his children Jem and Dill, (when judging Bo the feared neighbour), to 'always put yourself in the other persons skin'. It's a good exercise. Try it. Imagine yourself in another person's skin and your heart may just soften. It always works for me. I personally cannot tolerate injustice in life. And I have to speak up. Finding my voice and using it, doesn't necessarily change the world or even the situation but it usually makes me feel a whole lot better.

Having completed the basic training, national service stretched on. I became the fresh scapegoat. My discharge date of September 19th 1955 at 8am seemed a lifetime away. But, as always, I found a way to survive and turn round a sour situation. I'd been putting that theory into practice since my childhood days as an evacuee or boarder. The key to surviving national service was simple. All I had to do to make my daily life several notches more pleasurable was to join a sports squad.

"It gets you out of all duties," I was told by one of the trainees called Freddie Trueman. "Join the rugby team Bob. They need players".

I listened hard and respected his advice. Freddie was already an established sportsman, playing cricket for Yorkshire. He was well on his way to gaining a place in the English team. I was impressed and wanted to follow in his footsteps and join any national service team that would have me. My only concern was that I had little experience on the rugby pitch. Football had been my sport. I didn't let this little hiccup hold me back.

"Need any extra players?" I asked one of the rugby lads the following day. Looking me up and down he asked me the crucial question.

"You used to playing in a rugby team?" he replied. I nodded enthusiastically. " I'm . . . er. . . used to playing in a team,"

I confirmed. It was not a complete lie. Just a touch of bending the truth. I was used to being a team player. A football team player. That would surely do.

I joined the squad immediately and managed to convince everyone that I had almost been born with a rugby ball in my hands. Rugby was the best thing that came from National Service. Possibly, the only good thing.

Like Freddie, I was quickly excused from trivial tasks and bullying corporals. Instead, I got stuck into the scrums, fun and laughs. The rugby team even had our own planes and pilots to fly us up and down the country to any away matches. This was the life!

Match days were magic. The thought of them kept me going all week. We were usually commissioned at least two pilots who were keen to build up their flying hours and allowances. Not only were they good in the air, but a great addition to the ground squad as well.

These pilots would go from cockpit to changing room in the bat of any eyelid and then, of course, into the bar. Being in the rugby team naturally involved drinking beer. Whether we'd won, lost, played astoundingly well or performed abysmally, there was always time for a post match pint or three. Our pilots were usually first at the bar. They always ignored the drink-driving rule and didn't just wet their whistle but gave it a soaking. Finding a sober pilot to transport us back to camp was impossible. We had no choice but to put our lives into the hands of a drunk. Tanked up on alcohol, the chosen man would sink back in the cockpit, a smile on his ruddy face while we all said our private prayers.

"We're owf, " he'd grin as he pulled the throttle back and picked up speed on the runway. Airborne, I'd sit behind him all the way, making sure he didn't succumb to a booze induced late afternoon nap.

"Just relax Parsons," he'd grin, completely inebriated. "There's not much traffic up here."

I felt about as relaxed as any passenger would be with a half-cut pilot. If I could have flown the plane home myself - I would have done. Unfortunately, piloting a plane was not part of my

Chapter 10

national service training. Nor was dancing. I wished I had had both skills, as once a month, a dance was held in the NAAFI.

The local girls joined us. Lots of them. They decorated the dance hall like bunches of freshly picked daffodils. They were a sweet bunch. Quite shy but the occasional look from a pair of twinkling female eyes, kept us all going for weeks. To be able to move my feet in the right direction and boast I could fly a plane would have been more than a bonus with these women.

My ballroom lessons in Balham helped a little. But I had no training for any other form of dance. Rock 'n' Roll often dominated the evening. I loved the beat, the rhythm, the music and its stylish singers. But I was not a natural Buddy Holly, Bill Hayley or Elvis. I didn't have any blue suede shoes. My short, back and sides would not have suited the greased back look. I could only stand on the sidelines, envious of any mates who could grab a girl and shake, rattle and roll. In those moments I usually grabbed a beer and looked for a friendly face to chat up. Unfortunately, the best faces were usually far more interested in watching the floorshow than listening to my small talk. I didn't let it get me down. Well, not too much. I convinced myself it would be pointless to get mixed up with a girl as I was soon going to be demobbed. I had almost done my time.

11

Decisions

Forty-five years loyal service, an insincere handshake and a gold watch. Was that what I wanted in life?

September 19th 1955. I remember it well. It was the day I hung up my RAF beret, walked out of national service, and back into my life in Balham. I was destined for a career in print. My whole life was mapped out before me. I would finish my training at Wightman's, step into a set of management shoes, chalk up decade after decade of loyalty with the company and then collect a gold watch when I reached the finishing post in my retirement. That was the path ahead and just what my parents wanted for their son. It would be a good, safe, steady life. Wouldn't it? Something was niggling me.

I'd watched one of my work colleagues, Alf Mead reach retirement. He'd been with the company since he came out of short trousers. He was part of the furniture and for five days a week for fifty years he had devoted his life to Wightman's. For that half-century sentence, he got his watch, a handshake, a round of applause and his five minutes of company fame. On Friday at 5.30pm he picked up his briefcase and walked out the door with a smile of satisfaction on his face. On Monday, out of habit and boredom, he returned. Instead of being given the respect he deserved, he received a cold shoulder and a few harsh words from the young manager who had swiftly claimed his desk and duties. Alf was clearly not welcome or wanted on the premises anymore. It was cruel to witness his almighty crash down to earth and reality. Alf died of a broken heart six

Chapter 11

months after his retirement. Was I prepared to give my time, my heart and my life to Wightmans? I didn't need that gold watch. I had a perfectly good silver Timex.

For a year or three I knuckled down with the company and spent a year training in Lewes learning everything I would need to know about making money for the company and being a manager. I returned to the London office, joined the union, (the only person in management who did so), commuted daily, kept smiling, kept working hard and kept wondering whether I could accept this daily routine for the rest of my days. Spending hours standing up in an overfull underground carriage each week seemed such a waste of time. What's more, Wightman's didn't exactly fill me up with job satisfaction. Dad urged me to stay on the printing path. He was proud of me. I was searching for more.

I'd given up on the Chelsea squad dream. Instead, I founded the Ramsden Sports Club. Members filtered through from the Boys Brigade. We were a keen bunch – pulling together to enter the local cricket and football leagues or taking time out to watch the occasional Surrey game at the Oval. We also turned our energy to the more unusual game of rugby netball that can still be found on Clapham common today. It's the only place in the world where you will find this sport in action.

Ramsden Rugby Netball team, 1956. I'm on the back row, far right.

Despite all this sport and distraction I was forever hungry for a more satisfying career path. Just when I least expected it, the tide turned.

A pal of mine, Stuart Palmer, who I met playing football at weekends, seemed to have a far more interesting job than mine. It wasn't his wages that attracted me but what he did for a living. He didn't make big profits for a company. Instead he tried to make life just a little bit better for a few people. Stuart worked as a probation officer. I'd heard him talk about his work. It made me curious to know more. "How was your week?" I would ask him. And when he unfolded the ins and outs of his working days and the people he saw, met and tried to help, my eyes were opened wide. My job, in comparison seemed duller than watching paint dry slowly.

"Come and have a day as a probation officer," he said noticing my enthusiasm. I agreed. That one-day changed my life.

Stuart took me to East Dulwich in London to visit a few families he'd been assigned to help. Poverty, abuse and crime, was as regular in their lives as drinking a cup of tea. I met criminals, a mother with 16 children and barely sixpence in her pocket to feed them all, I saw kids that had suffered neglect and sexual abuse, and fathers who had nothing in their lives except booze and debt. It shocked me. I felt I was in the middle of one of those little glass snowstorm scenes just waiting to be shaken. When the snow settles, you know you will be in a slightly different picture and nothing can ever be just the same as it was before. In my entire semi-sheltered life, I had never stared such desperation in the face. These people were judged by some as the underclass of society that many people would conveniently pour down the drain. They had very little hope in life. And very little help. My heart went out to them.

I had been touched. Moved. Made to think. But if my dad had been able to read my mind, he would not have been pleased. I felt certain that I could not stay at Wightman's. I realised I wanted to do more with my life. And what's more I wanted to do more for other peoples lives. I knew what I had to do. I was going to jump ship, take up training as a welfare officer and then graduate to become a probation officer. Financially

Chapter 11

I would lose but it was almost what I could describe as 'a calling'. My conscience and heart were waking up and tapping me on the shoulder. Dad was not amused.

"You've got to be bloody joking," he snapped, when I told him I had been accepted on a training course for the probation service.

"You're throwing away a good job. A good career. Where's the sense in that?"

It made perfect sense to me. I was going to take out a loan to cover my studies, I would get my head down for a year, train, qualify, and hopefully get a job at the end of it. I knew it would be a struggle, but I would manage. It was the closest I could get to the university education I would only obtain much later, in the more mature years of my life.

Predictably, dad was outraged. One of the disadvantages of being an only child is that the only focus in the family was on me. I took the brunt of my parents' worries. I was the sole receiver of their angst, and anger. But however cross dad appeared at my career change, there was no way I would let him talk me out of my decision to leave Wightman's.

I handed in my notice. It went down about as well as Chelsea getting thrashed 5-0 at home. This company had invested money in my future. They could not believe that I was prepared to give it all up for uncertainty.

"Are you sure?" they asked.

Sure? I was 150% certain. In fact, when I walked out of the door of Wightman's for the very last time, I was tempted to leap in the air and kick my heels together or do a lap of honour round the block. I thought of Mao Tse Tung's words. *A journey of a thousand miles begins with a single step.* I knew I had done the right thing.

12

Wedding Bells

I was infatuated by the feminine mystique. Buxom was in vogue. Jane Russell and Marilyn Monroe were top of my list, but a curvaceous dark haired choir member at church was third. Her name was Ann Baker. She was soon going to become Ann Parsons.

Wearing a smile so wide it was almost impossible to squeeze it through the church doors, my fiancé Ann Baker walked down the aisle of Bonneville Baptist Church in Clapham on 24th September 1960, a leap year! I was waiting at the altar. My best man, Paul Turner beside me.

"You've got one minute to call the whole thing off and marry me," Paul teased.

I'd been dating Ann for two years before we tied the knot. We met at the local church. Ann was in the choir. I was in the congregation. I didn't care whether she had the voice of an angel or a voice that could curdle milk. I was just charmed by her gentle ways, the spark in her eyes, her alluring curves, and more than impressed that she was happy to chat me up. My shyness and lack of self-esteem went straight out the church window. Perched in the pews, I would peep up from my hymnbook and from the corner of my eye I would watch Ann singing her heart out with the choir. Church had never been so much fun. After the service we would share a cuppa and a rich tea biscuit, then chitchat about members of the congregation and the latest gossip. The tea and the chat were not important. What mattered to me was the opportunity to move a step closer to the opposite sex. As far as I was concerned girls came from another planet. Talking to Ann was the personal equivalent of jumping on Star Trek's 'Enterprise' spaceship, orbiting space and getting the chance to 'boldly go where I'd never been before'.

We drifted into a relationship. It was as smooth as melted chocolate. We got along without trying too hard. Courting was done properly. Decently. Politely. There was no other way at that time in life, or if there was, I didn't hear about it. Sex before marriage in the fifties, was about as likely as going to the moon. At least that's what I'd been told.

I was happy with Ann by my side. Sometimes we went for a drink together, on other days, I'd woo Ann with a ride in my clapped out dark red Austin Seven old banger. I felt like a Lord in that motor.

It was my very first car. It cost me all of fifteen hard earned pounds. But it cost me a lot more in repairs. I lost count of the number of times I had to roll my sleeves up, open the bonnet and try to fix the engine. But when it worked it was glorious. Sitting behind the wheel with Ann by my side, I'd smile at the world and hope and pray we reached our destination. We enjoyed our four wheeled excursions. We were young. We were in love. We were hardly Posh and Becks but we didn't need wealth, designer labels, the latest fashion, fast cars and fabulous haircuts to keep us happy. Just a clapped out car, a chance to hold hands and a bag of chips to share at the end of an evening.

Mum and dad warmed to Ann. Shebe did too. Our dating continued. We were 'going steady' and I knew I was on the right path in life with Ann. Mum felt the same. I could sense she had well and truly accepted Ann and was keen to play an active part in planning the wedding. First I had to do the right thing and ask Ann's father if I could marry his daughter. I was nervous. But determined.

Ann's parents, Louise and Bill Baker had already given me the once over on numerous occasions. They were true blues. And that didn't mean they supported Chelsea. But the political opposition. I hoped politics didn't stand in the way of my future.

"I'd like your permission to marry your daughter," I boldly asked Mr Baker. For a second he hesitated. Then nodding with approval, he shook my hand. The wedding was on.

"We're getting married," I announced to my parents over Sunday dinner. We celebrated on a sherry. Shebe did well for scraps that afternoon.

But before wedding bells rang, I was keen to follow tradition and organise a stag night event. I didn't want the usual drunken get-together in the pub. Instead, I opted to have a boy's only stag holiday adventure. Two tandems, four chaps and three countries were on the agenda. Wally, Paul and another great pal, Eric Palmer accompanied me. We rode on two rickety tandems, laughing all the way through France, Belgium and Luxembourg. I tried out my schoolboy French. Paul tried out his animal magnetism on a few of the very forthcoming French girls. We returned, a few flat tyres later very tired, very broke but men of the world! I was ready to tie the knot.

Tandem tearaways, France. From left, Wally, me and Paul.

Chapter 12

So Ann slipped into a long white wedding dress and became Mrs Parsons. And I stepped into my one and only suit and became a little bit tipsy. We celebrated our big day at the nearby unglamorous Bedford Pub with a buffet and a bit of a knees up. It was a heart-warming occasion. Paul gave a great speech. He told our guests all about the many girlfriends I had pulled over the years! I smiled, mum cried a little; dad drank a lot and Wally, dear Wally, my childhood pal from the streets of Balham kept smiling. It really was a day to remember. When the last dance was over and the guests had trickled off home, Paul chauffeured us to a West End hotel for the evening, a trail of old tin cans rattling behind his car.

"They're not really married," he cheekily told the hotel proprietors as he carried our suitcases into the hotel. Ann blushed gently and giggled. We kept the smiles on our faces, enjoying the attention and the luxury of hotel accommodation. The next day we caught a ferry to France for our honeymoon. The sea was choppy. We didn't care. We were Mr and Mrs Parsons now.

Wedding day

Married life began in a terraced home in middle class Norbury, South London. For £2,200 we had a garden and the luxury of an inside toilet. I'd gone up a notch in life. But we struggled to pay the mortgage. There was no extra money for luxuries. Our furniture had been begged borrowed, hopefully not stolen. Most of it needed to be held together with sticky tape. Our prize possession was a second-hand twelve-inch black and white television. It had an irritating, intermittent fault and needed a sharp bang on the top when the picture went astray.

Every evening when we sat down for the evenings viewing I had the all-important job of applying a touch of brute force to our television. If you hammered it too hard the picture would be lost forever. Too soft and it remained a fuzz of black and white snow. But with the right heavy handed touch, programmes could be restored. The television had a habit of breaking down right in the middle of our favourite programme – 'That was the week that was'. Sometimes we had to guess the punch line.

We were content in our two up – two down television bashing terrace. Ann continued her job, working as a secretary to a solicitor in the City. And I was quite literally sent to Coventry for three months, to begin my training as a probation officer. Lodging by week, and returning home by weekend I stepped into my new career path. Slowly.

I had entered another world. A world of problems. A world of the underclass. It was an intense time, absorbing their daily worries, meeting and mixing with 'problem families' who seemed to have very little chance to dig themselves out of their deep holes. I remember visiting a young single parent on probation. Her crime had been shoplifting. She was in a terrible drug induced mental state, and stood wide-eyed, helpless vigorously rocking her young baby dangerously close to the open window of her fourth floor flat. What could I do for this woman? I offered to hold her baby. I called for a doctor. Did her baby need to go into care? What chance did mum or baby have in life?

Another young lad who had been caught housebreaking justified his behaviour to me. "I only rob from the people that

Chapter 12

have money," he explained. Robin Hood may have got away with it, but this youth wouldn't.

I clearly remember preparing a court report for David, a twelve-year-old lad who was charged with destroying 2000 flowers in a local park. Meeting the boy and his family at home explained everything about his behaviour. He had six brothers and a pregnant 15-year-old sister. The mother was also pregnant by a neighbour. In the corner of the urine smelling living room, a baby screamed endlessly from the depths of a dirty pram and the second youngest boy of the family mated my leg as I stood in the middle of the chaos, interviewing the family. David had a bad stammer. He wet his bed frequently. He played truant regularly and was the scapegoat at school.

This was not a picture of happy families. It was no wonder David had let his emotions loose on the local flowerbed. David was put on probation for two years which entailed working with all members of the family to help steer him clear from a life of crime. It was hard to walk away from David and other clients at the end of the working day. Like ghosts, they haunted me at night. At Wightman's as soon as my working day was over, I left my work worries behind. In my new training I was taking my stress home.

On the weekends when I returned to Ann, I could not help but offload the woes of the week. She did her best to listen but she simply could not understand the pressures of my job. I had to find another way to deal with my working life. The solution was simple. I joined the London Scottish rugby squad.

Scrums, mud, men and eighty tough minutes of physical exercise every Saturday was a great antidote to the mental and emotional stress. Running up and down the pitch, I'd offload the weight that was on my shoulders. It always worked. Yet when the final whistle blew my mind immediately switched to football. I was keen to see the match results of the day out in print. Kicking the mud off my boots, I'd race to the street corner to wait for the newspaper van to thump bundles of its latest edition of the News, Star or Standard onto the pavement. There was something very thrilling about the rush to find out the scores. Parting with my pennies, I'd grab the freshly printed pink-paged paper, lick my muddy fingers and excitedly turn to the sports section.

The Chelsea result was a priority. If a win was reported I'd be more than happy. It was the closest I could get to being back at Stamford Bridge. A loss meant a brief inner sulk. Although I much preferred to play sport at this time in my life than be a spectator, I was still devoted to Chelsea. My veins were Chelsea blue. The more goals we scored, the stronger the colour of my veins. Sometimes I'd visit dad on the way home to discuss our shared passion.

"How did Chelsea get on?" he'd eagerly ask as soon as I stepped foot in the door. Grabbing the paper out of my hand, he'd turn to the crucial back pages to study the match report and racing results. He knew by the look on my face if Chelsea had got their two points. Like me, football was part of his life. Mum remained uninterested in football, but was always pleased to see me home.

"You'll have had your tea before you came?" she would joke in a broad Scottish accent. It was her way of inviting me to share some food and a cuppa. Warming the chipped brown pot, she'd make a brew for us all. Mum was feeling my absence at home. Dad still had greyhounds, his football results, the pub and his working life. Mum's days were simply centred on the home and domestic chores. It had always been that way. You never saw dad near the kitchen sink or cooker. That was woman's work and mum's department. It was the same for every woman in the street. The men were the breadwinners. The women were the bread makers. The men socialised. The women stayed at home. Apart from visiting her sisters, mum had very few people in her life. This 'unbalanced' way of living seemed to work well for my parents. But occasionally, there was tension in the air and dad would throw his daily frustrations her way.

He didn't mince his words. He was a man who spoke his mind. He'd had plenty of practice over the years at labour party and union meetings. Mum could certainly hold her own, but would look wounded when dad's temper got the better of him. Sometimes, he ignored her completely and turned his attentions to Shebe or the new addition to the household -

Chapter 12

Scruff. Dear Scruff was a dog who lived up to her name and I suspect was my four legged replacement. She was there to fill the gaps and silences. Of course, she could not talk football. But she could listen to dad without answering back. That was what he wanted. No wonder man's best friend is his dog!

"He's always talking to the dogs, but he ignores me," mum would complain. And out of the corner of my eye I'd spot dad mischievously chatting away to his cherished canines, fuelling the tensions and stirring up mum.

Such behaviour visibly upset mum. The occasional tears would flow and I would automatically step in to defend her. My loyalties to mum stretched back to the war years when it was just the two of us against the world. That closeness I would never forget. Since I had left home it seemed mum and dads marriage was being tested. I became the go-between. The closest they could get to marriage guidance. I tried to bridge the small gap that had come between them. Divorce, splitting up or separating was never on the agenda. It was not a common option in the early 60's, nor was it something either of them wanted. My parents, like so many other couples accepted their differences, continued with their arguments and simply got on with the ups and downs of married life.

Dad was still grieving for the job I gave up at Wightman's and still struggling to come to terms with the decision I had made.

"How's the probation service training?" he would politely ask. But he wasn't really interested. I knew he had little time for other people's problems. As far as he was concerned depression, debt, and being disadvantaged in life, could all be sorted out with a bit of hard graft.

"They've brought it all on themselves," he would argue, refusing to feel sorry for anyone. "Its their own fault."

Dad, I suspected would never change his point of view. I did not try and argue but simply continued on the path I had chosen in life. I knew it was the right one. With Ann by my side - loyal, true and always very supportive I could take a few more "steps" to reach my goals in life.

13

Double Joy

On March 26th 1963, our first child Graeme Stephen was born in the upstairs bedroom of our Norbury home in Strathyre Avenue. The very next day I sat my final exams for the probation service. Three months later, we moved out of London to start a new life in Hemel Hempstead. Life was rapidly changing. For the better.

First came the labour pains. Then came the midwife, the doctor and my anxious mother-in-law. A baby was on the way. And all I could do was stand back and let the women get on with the job they know best.

I was about to become a father. My emotions were on a roller coaster ride. Up. Down. Shaky. Euphoric. Exhilarating. Fearful. I could not wait to be a dad, but just like my own father, I was worried by the huge responsibility that lay ahead. Pacing the four corners of the living room, the main concern on my mind was that my baby would be born healthy.

Graeme was in no rush to come into the world. He kept me waiting, and pacing, and waiting and pacing. But as soon as the midwife called my name I was in the biggest rush of my life to see my baby.

"It's a boy," Ann beamed. My heart jumped for joy. Peeping at the fresh newborn I smiled proudly. I had a son. A wonderful child to love and nurture. My wee lad had made me a dad. Happy was an understatement. The joy in my heart far

Chapter 13

exceeded Chelsea winning every trophy in the land. I was a father. I had a baby. Ten fingers. Ten toes. A sweet face and a cry that almost stopped my heart.

But I barely had time to hold my boy before I was running off the next day to take my probation service exams. I'd studied the theory and experienced the practical parts of the course. Now it was time to prove on paper that I was ready for the job. I felt confident. Important lessons had been learnt in my training period. Three months had been spent in Coventry, three more at the Family Service Unit in Islington and a final chapter of my training had taken place in Hemel Hempstead. Over the course of a year, my eyes had been opened wide.

Drugs, rape, abuse, alcohol, crime, paedophilia, prostitution, family breakdown, homelessness, unemployment and mental health problems had all gone past me on the conveyor belt of life. I'd absorbed it all. Seen it in the raw. Touched it. Felt it. Smelt it and tried to do something constructive about the problem.

In 12 months I'd seen more of life than I'd seen in my thirty years. I'd been on a placement at Wandsworth prison, talked to offenders, and prison officers. I'd been out for a night with the homeless, finding out for myself the reality of sleeping rough. Waterloo car park, in the cold and rain at 4am, was an experience I was glad I did not have to repeat. But it gave me insight and empathy. I attended the funeral of a man who had spent fifty-seven of his seventy-one years in prisons and institutions. He knew no other life. He had started as a petty criminal, thieving milk from doorsteps but had got so used to prison life; he would plan his next offence before he had even been released. I was the only person at his funeral. Just me, the coffin and an empty church.

As well as soaking up the underbelly side of life, I had also learnt how to cope with it all. Emotionally, the probation service can be draining. But I had acquired the necessary skills to remain strong, constructive and positive. Now, it was time to gain the much-needed qualification. I was more than determined to pass. There was no turning back.

"Good luck," Ann grinned, as I got ready to leave the house

and head to Sloane Square for my three-hour exam papers. Kissing my sons soft downy hair I picked up my books and lunchbox and left the house. As I walked purposefully through the Norbury streets, a big part of me wanted to tell the world and every passer-by that I was a father. The other part of me just wanted to focus completely on the test ahead. I was ready for fatherhood. I was ready for this exam. I hoped I would do well in both but I would have to wait ten anxious days to hear my results. Baby Graeme kept my mind busy and the exam worries at bay.

Ann loved every minute as a mum. Although she was weary, she was glowing with pride every time she held her baby boy. My parents felt the same. Dad was absolutely delighted to have a grandson to follow in his footsteps, mum was equally happy, although I did suspect she was secretly longing for a little girl.

It was a busy time. Stepping into the role of being a dad took time. I wasn't exactly a 'hands-on nappy changing, rock the baby through the night type of father,' but I did my bit. One morning, while Ann was busy settling Graeme, my exam results dropped through the letterbox.

Pausing for just one second, I prepared myself to open the envelope. Was it going to be good news? What would I do if I'd failed? There was no way I could turn the clocks back and with tail between my legs, retreat to Wightman's. To my relief, I had passed my exams. Bursting with joy, I broke the news to Ann and Graeme. He wasn't listening but Ann was delighted for me. It was time to apply for jobs.

"There's a vacancy in Watford," I told Ann later that week "Shall I apply?"

Watford was just a 10-minute train ride from the new town of Hemel Hempstead where I had done a three-month placement during my training. I had been impressed with Hemel and the way it had been carefully planned. The newly constructed homes, the green grass of playing fields and the wide-open spaces were a great contrast to Norbury and my childhood streets of Balham. Hemel Hempstead, I felt sure would be an ideal place to bring up children.

Chapter 13

I was keen for my son to grow up with good schools, good facilities and some nature on his doorstep. Hemel had all these things and . . . quite a few promising looking pubs.

Within three months of Graeme's birth, we were on the move. Not in a silver cross pram as my dad had used when I was a baby, but in the back of my old banger. I had been offered the Watford job. I was about to step into the shoes of being a probation officer. A new job had prompted us to buy a £2,650 home in Hemel Hempstead, a new town an hour from the heart of London.

Our new house was a semi detached in Ridge Lea. We had a front and back garden, an indoor loo, bathroom, three bedrooms, a big living room and of course our baby boy to fill the home with love and laughter. We had everything.

I started my new job with Watford probation service just days after moving in. It was more than a job. It was a major part of my life that I quickly grew to love. I had joined a unique team. They were an amazing, first class bunch of professionals who gave their heart, time and energy to their job. We worked long hours. Our caseload was heavy. But thanks to team spirit and the guidance of a very supportive senior, Tom Burke, we kept the wheels turning. Together we got the job done and reached for our goals.

One of my other work mates, Stuart Rees was an inspiration. He went the extra mile in the course of his working day and tried to make life an inch better for every one of his clients. Many of them were children who had endured years of physical, mental or sexual abuse. He gave himself to every one of them. I did the same. Every week I would spend at least two days in the Magistrates Court preparing the Pre-Trial Enquiry Reports in the cells. We called them 'Magic Eyes'. They allowed the magistrates to have additional information on the unrepresented defendants. Being 'banged up' with the offenders was an interesting, memorable experience. I lost count of the number of times I was asked "can you give us a fag Guv?"

I remember one young offender I visited in the cells had been accused of having unlawful sexual intercourse (USI) with a girl under the age of 16. He was 18. His girlfriend was 15. Both of them were immature and came from a rural area. In court, they struggled verbally.

"Have you had sexual intercourse?" The Chair of the Bench asked the awkward looking girl. Upon the advice of her solicitor she had been asked to dress in school uniform in order to look as young as possible.

"What's sexual intercourse?" the girl replied, genuinely confused. "I don't know what that means." The Chair scratched his head and tried again.

"Have you slept together," he asked, hoping this time he would be understood. No such luck. The girl paused, shook her head and crossed her eyebrows.

"Me mum wont let me have friends in my bedroom to sleep," she replied. This case was going nowhere slowly and was on the verge of turning into a comedy sketch. When I had interviewed the boy, he confessed they had sex in the haystack and that the girl looked so much older in make up and a mini skirt than she did in school uniform. He received a conditional discharge.

Times have certainly changed. Teenage sex is the norm nowadays and very few USI cases are brought to court.

In the courtroom it was often my job to stand up and give evidence. As a Quaker, I did not take the oath but affirmed. Some of the magistrates were suspicious with this variation from the norm.

Several months into my new job, Stuart and I were revolutionary in setting up probation camps for 12 – 14 year olds. Our proposal caused many tongues to wag in the probation service. It was something that had never been done before. But we were determined to take a group of needy teenagers for a week under canvas in Dover.

The project was risky. These youths had not come from middle class mild mannered backgrounds. They had been exposed to crime and abuse. A group of them, running wild and free in Dover, could spell trouble. These kids knew how to fight, steal, shout and stomp. Witnessing the harsh side of life hardened their young faces. But I was confident the probation camp would do them good. Tough outer shells are often just in place to fool the world. Once you get beneath the layers of thick

Chapter 13

skin, you usually find a warm heart in desperate need of love, affection and attention.

We knew the week in Dover would be more than a challenge. But every struggle brings rewards. At least that's what we believed. That's what we kept telling ourselves as we boarded the mini buses and headed south. The kids sang all the way. Their spirits were soaring. I was optimistic that they would not give us too much trouble.

The campsite was a fifteen-minute walk from the sea. The sun was shining that day and so were the campers. Tents were erected. Wood was collected. Food was purchased and a rota was drawn up for cooking duties. A bonus for the boys was the chance to run their own tuck shop. It could have backfired. All supplies of sweets, crisps, drinks and the small float of money could have been swiftly stolen and consumed. But, these lads rose to the responsibility. Not a single item went missing. In contrast, on a day trip to Calais, the group were keen to take back anything and everything French. They just weren't so keen to pay for it. Unbeknown to me, pockets were filled as France was invaded. It seemed almost every child went home with a free French souvenir. "Merci beaucoup" was the phrase of the day. No wonder the boys were smiling. The haul was brought back to camp and the boys confessed. But more importantly than the shoplifting that had taken place, was the memory of a great day.

So many young faces had lit up as the ferry majestically glided across the sea from one country to the next. Many of these lads had never witnessed the power of the waves. They had never been given the chance to visit the coast, and experience the simple joy of throwing pebbles in the sea or dipping a toe in the water. Visiting France had been about as likely in their daily lives, as taking a rocket to the moon. It was an exhilarating experience for them all. Although they remained rowdy in their week away, they generally respected the rules, played fair and square and returned home with a week of top memories.

Accompanying us for the week was a Kenyan probation officer trainee. He certainly stood out from the crowd with his impeccable dress code. While we all wore shorts and t-shirts, he spent the week in a suit and tie, looking every inch an English gent. It gained him respect, raised a few eyebrows and a few laughs.

"Haven't you got any shorts?" the boys would laugh. "Do you wanna borrow mine?" "Who do you think you are - Prince Charles?"

So the week ran as smoothly as possible until, on the last day of camp, one lad went missing. It was a worrying moment. We searched the campsite and shouted his name. Thirty minutes later I was more than anxious. I prayed nothing had happened to him. Then out of the corner of my eye, I spotted the absconder. . . . not running away across the fields or rowing out to sea, but perched comfortably up a nearby tree and watching us from above.

"You coming down," I asked him casually. "We're ready to leave." Shaking his head he simply replied, "I don't want to go home."

Who could blame him? He'd probably just experienced the best week of his life. He'd felt the wind in his hair, the salt water on his skin, he'd run free, he'd cooked on an open fire, slept under canvas and smoked a packet or two of French cigarettes. He had laughed daily. Eaten daily. Why would he want to return to the step-dad who had never accepted him or respected him? Why would he want to settle back into a home where physical abuse was part of his daily life?

I like to think that this camp and the two more that followed, may have changed these children just a little. I like to hope that it gave them the opportunity to experience life and help them find a way to cope with their problems. Perhaps, like me, some of those campers still look back and remember that week in Dover. Stuart certainly reminisces on these probation camps from time to time. His path in life took him from Watford to Aberdeen, Canada and Australia where he founded the Centre for Peace Studies at Sydney University. He, and his dear wife Ragnhild, have remained loyal friends over the years and are godparents to my children. We keep in touch. We look back with fond memories. Mainly, we try to look forward.

14

"It's a Girl"

I was sent out to get a loaf of bread. When I returned, my dear daughter Kathryn Susan had made her grand entry into the world. Our family was complete.

She was born at home on March 6th 1965 while I was out shopping. By the time I had returned and unlocked the front door, I could hear her soft cries coming from the bedroom upstairs and Ann was sitting propped up in bed looking more content than the cat that got the cream. We had a baby girl. Kathryn Susan Parsons. A blonde haired baby sister for Graeme. I was a lucky man. We had two healthy children to love and guide in life. I put the lunch on. A feast of sausages, chips and peas. Later that afternoon, leaving Ann, Graeme and Kathryn in the capable arms of my mum I went off to play rugby for the local team – Camelot. Elation and exhaustion ran through my veins. I didn't know which way I was kicking. We lost. But I was a winner that day.

In the days and weeks that followed, neighbours called round to take a peep at the baby. I welcomed them all. They were a great bunch of people. Our cul-de-sac was, and still is, a real community. There was a strong camaraderie. In the early 60's, we were all relatively new to Hemel Hempstead. Like me, many families had come from London to begin a new life "in the new town".

We helped each other settle in. We even shopped communally, pooling our money to buy in bulk. Sometimes we purchased loo rolls, other times we got a pig from the local farm and everyone went home with the bacon. It made sense to come together. Our children were going to be growing up in the same turning, taking the same route to nursery and primary school. It was important that friendships were forged. We were Hemel's answer to a Kibbutz.

The neighbourhood homed an interesting cocktail of characters. One couple ran nudist parties, another household consisted of two men and one woman all living happily together (no questions asked), then there were the retired pensioners who seemed to go on holiday almost every month of the year and the elderly neighbour who was locked out daily by his wife. Whatever the weather he was not allowed to smoke his cigars in the house and would have to take a morning stroll to the nearby park to puff and inhale to his hearts content. One of the most popular neighbours on the block was Den, an expert home brewer. He kept the cul-de-sac happy with his constant supplies of elderflower wine. In return I bottled pickled onions using a special family recipe and method handed down over the years. My uncle Charlie had passed on the secret formula to me. I have handed it over to the next chosen pickler, my cousin Colin Steele, the son born to Uncle Charlie after he was discharged from army service.

Ann had many good mates in the neighbourhood. Mums seemed to congregate together, support each other and care for each other's kids. Ann was a hardworking natural mother. She knew the reason behind every sniff, whimper and cry and how best to deal with it. Graeme's teething troubles could be soothed, and Kathryn's hunger cries could be met. I was continually astounded.

Mothers are incredible. Around the world, the mums I have continued to meet have never ceased to amaze me. Living in difficult conditions, and surviving on the most meagre wages, not only do they raise the children, but they collect the wood, sell their wares on the market, work the fields and prepare food.

It's not uncommon in Sri Lanka to see one baby strapped to a mother's front, while she plucks tea from plantations depositing the leaves in a large basket on her back. It is always

Chapter 14

the mothers who seem to work the hardest and then use their reserves to put things right in the family unit.

Ann was always putting things right in our Ridge Lea home. When Kathryn was just six months old, Ann's maternal instincts proved to be lifesaving. Baby Kathryn fell ill. She had a temperature. Her breathing was strained.

"She's not well," Ann said pacing the room. "She's not right. She needs a doctor now." We called our family GP, Dr Sutton. He came. He examined our daughter. He went. Thank goodness his instincts kicked in. Ten minutes later he returned. Anxiety was imprinted on his face.

"I've treated a case very similar to this recently," he explained. "It may be meningitis." The diagnosis scared me. My heart thumped with fear and adrenalin kicked in. Within minutes, a neighbour was looking after Graeme and we were on our way to Hemel Hempstead hospital every second feeling like a day. In Ann's arms, in the back of the car, little Kathryn was fighting for her life. She was gasping for air. I prayed silently.

At the hospital, no time was wasted. Our baby girl was dashed into the operating theatre. We could only wait. The next twelve hours were crucial. The torture of being able to do nothing but hope, pray and will our daughter to be strong was a testing experience I would not wish on anyone. My emotions churned as I peered through the glass windows to see four surgeons and a gathering of nurses standing over our baby. Together, they were trying to save her life. We were both in pieces. Minutes felt like days. I prayed again. The wait seemed like an eternity. Every second, and every minute dragged. I had to remain positive.

The relief was overwhelming when we were told that Kathryn was going to be all right. She was lucky. More than lucky. I was grateful to the doctor, grateful to the whole medical team, and thankful to the NHS. In my later years when I travelled to all corners of the globe, I visited countries where medical facilities are just not available. Children perish in these locations. They don't stand a chance when illness strikes.

My heart still hangs heavy when I remember witnessing a desperate father in Nepal who had carried his sick son for three days and nights through mountainous terrain in hope of finding medical treatment. Imagine walking or almost crawling for days and nights on end to get to the nearest doctor. Imagine taking your son or daughter on such a gruelling journey when they are already sick and suffering.

That determined dad did reach the medical centre. He did get to a doctor. Sadly he was too late. His son was too ill to survive. The boy died in the arms of the desperate father who had tried in vain to save him. There were no words that could comfort this grief stricken man. I felt his pain. I cannot forget him. Nor could I forget little Kathryn's brush with death. It had shaken me. She had survived the killer virus but it was both a miracle and a terrifying experience.

Yet, within a week in hospital, Kathryn was strong again and ready to come home. I took her lead and knuckled back down into my working life. My job had conveniently transferred to Hemel. I saved precious time travelling to work. But the hours were still long and even on my weekends and days off I frequently bumped into my clients around town. One of them a real rough diamond kind of geezer, went on to become a millionaire and made a welcome donation to the charity I would launch in later life.

I developed strong relationships with the Irish Travellers that lived in Hemel. There were at least fifteen families who would park up their caravans on the open fields that have now become Jarman Park Leisure Centre. A few of them liked a drink. One of them in particular - a wiry haired man with skin as tough as leather, liked quite a few drinks. His name was Finbar. Every time our paths crossed he would make the same drunken promise.

"I'm just going to take the pledge with Father Foster. This is my last drop of alcohol Mr Parsons. My last drop."

I'd lost count of the number of times he had taken the same pledge. I did not judge him. Like his friends, he always greeted me politely and I was made welcome in his humble caravan home. One of his mates – Miles, sometimes unexpectedly turned up on my doorstep. Although the probation service discouraged relationships outside of work, I'd open my door to him. Miles had a good heart. It was usually soaked in booze, but he meant well. He had five children and a wife who supported him through thick and thin. He cried when he was drunk. He laughed when he was sober. He had fingers in many pies. When I needed a piano shifted to my home, Miles made it happen.

"Don't you worry, I'll get that piano to you," he promised. He was a man of his word. The piano arrived. . . rattling along in the back of a horsebox. Thankfully, the horse wasn't in the box at the time. Four hefty men with tattooed arms, and the scent of whiskey, carried it into our home.

"I like to do things for Bob," Miles told them. A few weeks later, I helped Miles and some of his mates get their names on the housing list so they could move out of their caravans into a more permanent home. Others were living in temporary accommodation. Occasionally I would hear that they had been evicted and would be sleeping rough in the woods. I did what I could for them. They were not the most popular members of the local community.

Dad had little time and understanding for travellers or "gypos" as they were commonly labelled. He was anti gay, anti gypsy, anti so many things. But when it came to his two grandchildren he had all the time, love, and understanding in the world. He enjoyed his visits to Hemel and together with mum, he would arrive on the coach from London, a packet of roll ups in his pockets and his arms outstretched. For my parents, Hemel was the countryside and a welcome contrast to the streets of Balham.

"Its all changing back home," dad would say and he'd give me an update on my childhood haunts and surrounding areas. The Odeon had been closed down. The West Indian population was growing, and the Balham Theatre had become a bingo hall. Despite the wind of change, dad remained much the same. Football, the greyhounds and the pub were still a large part of his life. . and of course Shebe and Scruff.

15

Football Fever

We called ourselves Ridge Lea United. I was the manager, the trainer, the ref and the first aid man. The kids from the cul-de-sac made up the team. All shapes and sizes were welcome. We never won a match. It didn't matter.

Children of course, grow fast. Blink, and they suddenly sprout. One minute they are needy, dependant toddlers, tumbling around in nappies, and the next they are headstrong young characters with minds and opinions of their own. My son and daughter may have shared the same home, meals and influences but they were not two peas from the same pod. Graeme was a natural academic; Kathryn was a caring, practical child. Yet, the one thing they did both have in common with each other, and most of the local children, was having more energy than sense. I decided to try and harness that energy. I started a neighbourhood football team from a squad of just fourteen. Ridge Lea United was our name.

We did not discriminate against size, age, girls, boys or the ability to kick a ball. All you needed to be in the team was two legs, and the enthusiasm to turn up once a week for training. But putting a half reasonable team together was a challenge. Some kids just did not know which way to kick the ball. Others knew which way to kick but could not run, and some would be reduced to tears if they were not given the opportunity to play the full 90 minutes. We were not like any other team in the area. Neighbourhood clubs fought hard to be the best. We concentrated on being the best . . . losers.

Chapter 15

No matter how badly we performed, the parents turned out every weekend to proudly watch their kids. Community spirit became even stronger in those moments. Dads on the touchlines are more forceful and opinionated than a 50,000 strong crowd at Stamford Bridge. If their son or daughter was fouled, it could end in fisticuffs. If their child scored - then all heaven and earth moved. That didn't happen very often for Ridge Lea United. We knew how to lose well. But the dads found it hard to accept coming second.

Later, coaching the local rugby under 19s squad was another challenge that reaped more positive results than Ridge Lea United. On training nights I was accompanied by the family dog

Graeme and Kathryn with Smudge

– Smudge, a black and white Collie/ Spaniel cross bred variety of dog. She loved the rugby pitch and the encouraging support from the very small crowd that gathered on the weekends to watch the matches. Smudge was part of the squad. Wherever they went, she came too, wagging her tail and doing her best to attract any male dogs of the neighbourhood. Her mating escapades stopped many a scrum. It also helped her live to a ripe old age. She reached her twentieth birthday – which in dog years surely should gain her a place in the Guinness Book of Records for being around 140 human years old!

Sport in the community continued to beckon me. As well as running in the Hemel 10 miles and walking the Mayors 36 mile event with probationers, I turned my hand to assisting the local special needs swimming club – The Dolphins. One of my most satisfying times with The Dolphins was teaching a blind teenager to swim. Finding time for my own family was equally important and satisfying. When I wasn't managing Ridge Lea United I was accompanying Ann and the children to the Sunday gatherings at the Quaker Meeting House in Hemel. We were always welcomed and felt immediately at ease and at peace amongst the group. I enjoyed the Quaker way of looking at life and taking part in life. Quakers, or The Society of Friends believe in doing their part in the world to leave the next generation a similar record of work well done. Their 17th century founder – George Fox, said 'let your life speak.' They believe the reason they were put on earth is to help each other to make this a better world. 'Try to find the good in everyone,' is at the core of their thinking. It's a strong, positive philosophy that I have adopted and tried to apply over the years. I firmly believe there is good in every man. And this theory has constantly proved to be true. I have always tried my best to put it in place in my day-to-day life amongst my local community, as chair of the local Hostel for the Homeless, School Governor and when I was elected as a District and then County Councillor and later appointed as a Magistrate.

In my working week I was frequently brushing shoulders with so many outcasts of society. One of them was a man who had spent 48 years in prison. He could not stop breaking the law and had a long list of offences to his name.

At the ripe age of 65, on one of his brief moments of freedom, he met a woman he cared for. She felt the same way about him. He never returned to his old ways. That open-hearted woman obviously saw the good in him. She enabled him to let the better part of himself shine. He did not look back.

To witness just one individual giving up his bad habits and life of crime was good for my soul. I was constantly trying to find ways to help others turn their lives around. In Pentonville Prison, I helped to run an Alcoholics Anonymous Group. It was so popular that there was a waiting list to join. Every week more and more inmates turned up. Not because they wanted to quit boozing. But simply because of the cigarettes that were offered during the sessions. Not only did the AA group give them a break from their cells, but a fag as well. It cost me.

Gambling was the other addiction that caused so many offenders to go off the straight and narrow. I had one client, Michael who had a gambling problem. He also constantly forgot to pay his fines and rent and had accumulated huge debts. Michael owned two greyhounds. One of them was running in the Flapper Track final. He was certain to win. Michael decided to pawn his worldly possessions to raise as much money as he could to "put on the nose" and get himself straight with the winnings.

I was more than tempted to back the dog but my professionalism and probation service rules kicked in. I opted not to gamble. The dog predictably came in first. Michael should have been celebrating. Instead his head was hung low. At the last moment he had put his money on another uncertain dog. He just had to take a chance. It was a ridiculous decision. Michael lost everything. But he was not a bad man and he sent me an unexpected letter of appreciation years later. It was extremely rare to receive mail from probationers.

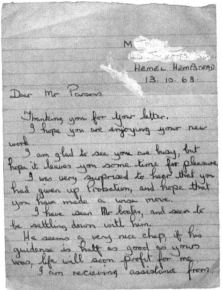

A letter from Michael

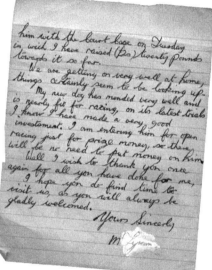

Working in the probation service, and trying to find the good in everyone broadened my horizons. I thankfully benefited from working under the old terms in which you were encouraged to 'advise, assist and befriend' clients. This system has since changed to a much more authoritative approach.

But those early years opened my eyes and mind wider than the Grand Canyon. Ahead of me were fresh challenges, new opportunities and strangers that would become good friends. I was on the right path in life. I just wasn't sure where that path would take me. But deep down inside, I felt sure my purpose in this life was to do the right thing for other people. That much was crystal clear.

Chapter 15

I was offered a post training probation officers and social workers in London. After much deliberation I decided to go with it.

16

Teaching Times

They called me Bob. I was their teacher, lecturer, their friend and the Course Director. There were one hundred mature students on each course intake and I wanted every single scholar to do well. What a responsibility. No wonder I took up smoking again!

Staff and students on the Social Work Training Course.
(I'm in the middle on the front row)

Teaching is satisfying. Passing on knowledge to those who are hungry to learn, is a rewarding role. For eight years I worked at North London Polytechnic as a lecturer and then Course Director. It was my job to run courses on Social Work. I was dedicated to my job and my students. They came from all walks of life. Mothers going back to work, the unemployed and those seeking a more satisfying career, were taking a new direction in life and returning to education. The government had implemented the Seebohm Report, which encouraged mature students to return to the classroom and pursue a career in social work. These students had much to offer. They

Chapter 16

had seen life, lived it and experienced its problems. It was my job to relate the theory to their life experiences. I did my best for every single student.

My workload was huge. Writing publications, essays and dissertations thousands of words long would need to be marked. Courses would need to be planned. Burning the midnight oil, I would cast my eye over assignments, and try to stay focussed. I took up smoking again. It helped me concentrate. Nicotine nights unfolded. My lungs took the brunt of the workload. I knew that a fifteen a day cigarette habit was not good for the family nor me. After twelve months of staining my fingers yellow, I decided it was time to quit the fags and devote more of my time to exercising Smudge.

"I will give you £1 for every cigarette I smoke after today," I announced to Graeme and Kathryn. They rubbed their hands with glee, certain that a few coins would be coming their way. I have never liked wasting money. To my delight but to the dismay of the children, I never touched another cigarette. I had beaten my addiction without having to part with a single penny.

I put my saved pennies and plenty more to better use by taking advantage of the long summer vacation and packing us all off on a four-week holiday to the USA and Canada. In America we rode from the East Coast to the West on a $99 Greyhound ticket making a final stop at the 1976 Montreal Olympics. My children came home with the travel bug running through their veins.

They were both slowly finding their direction in life. My son was a natural academic. From his early days as a pupil at Chaulden JMI school he had excelled in the classroom and had been offered a scholarship at Berkhamsted public school. The famous writer, Graham Greene had studied at the prestigious fee paying school, but Graeme Parsons, after much deliberation and consultation with his parents, declined the offer. Instead, he became a pupil at Cavendish Comprehensive School. It was the right decision. His intelligence shone through.

Graeme gained a good all round education and when it came

Graduation day for Graeme, Kathryn shares the moment

to making decisions about his future, I tried to steer him towards choosing medicine. Of course, very few children listen to their father's words of wisdom. My dad had dreamt I pursue a career in the print industry. I overturned his advice, and chose the probation service. I dreamt Graeme would become a doctor. I tried my hardest to tempt him towards a medical career. He opted to study history at Southampton University and gained a 2.1 BA degree.

Kathryn was more practical minded. She was bright, intelligent but needed to seriously put her head down in her books in order to pass exams. She was pulled towards teaching and was studying hard at Cavendish school to gain the necessary qualifications to put her on a path that would lead to a teaching degree at Leeds Polytechnic years later.

In what little spare time I had, I kept busy coaching the squad of twenty-five under 19 year olds in rugby. Our team was called Camelot Colts. We started slowly. Losing regularly. Within two years we had won the County Championship and cruised through a season completely unbeaten. From the training ground green fields of Hemel Hempstead we produced County and England International players. I was a proud man. I put time, effort and enthusiasm into training the squad. My contribution had paid off.

Meanwhile, off the rugby field, as the social work course

Chapter 16

The Camelot Colts

was running down. I did a part-time management course and embarked on gaining an MA at Brunel University as a part-time student, which was later to be converted into a Ph.D. I then became an Adviser on Social Work Training. But I was about to be pulled away from this career and take a new path in life. A job advert in 'New Society' magazine had attracted my attention. The vacancy was in Sri Lanka. The employer was *Save the Children*. The job involved setting up regional courses for trainers in Asia and establishing a recognized qualification for Child Care staff in Sri Lanka. I knew very little about Sri Lanka. But this job vacancy would not leave my thoughts. I had the necessary experience that the job required. I was curious. Interested. Drawn to the job and the country.

"Go for it," Ann said encouragingly when I showed her the advertised position. Taking her advice, I went for an interview. Walking into the room and facing a panel of professional people from the charity I felt confident. Walking out of the room, a sixty-minute interview over, I knew the job was mine.

17

New Horizons

Sri Lanka. 1982. Death, destruction and civil war would soon be on my doorstep. Working for *Save the Children*, I would be facing the biggest challenge of my life.

Easing into my seat, I fastened my safety belt, glanced out the window of the plane and silently said my goodbyes to England. I was bound for Sri Lanka. Flying into a new job, a new way of life and new horizons. I'd never stepped foot in any developing countries. My stomach was churning with nervous excitement.

Graeme, Kathryn and Ann had waved me off at the airport "Take care," they chorused. We hugged. Smiled. They let me go. I had done the same for them. They were firmly walking their own paths in life. Graeme was at Southampton University studying history. Kathryn was still at home finishing off her A levels, and Ann, after completing a B.Ed, was working as a youth leader. They had dreams and goals to strive towards. And I was on a two-year contract for *Save the Children*. My mission was to set up Child Care Training in Sri Lanka. It was a much-needed priority. The country was desperate to try and upgrade its care facilities. Orphanages were overcrowded and understaffed. My job was to establish a training scheme for the staff who were working in residential establishments with vulnerable children. The staff had been ignored and undervalued for too long. They required guidance, recognition, a status. Quite simply, they needed to be equipped with the skills and support necessary to look after the young and

Chapter 17

needy. With these things in place, the vulnerable children in their care would have a better life.

In the UK I had been plunged into all sorts of situations. I'd seen and touched the underbelly of life. But nothing had prepared me for the sight, smell and silences that lay behind the doors of some Sri Lankan orphanages and residential homes.

Place a large group of young children under one roof and you would expect to hear the sound of play, tears and hopefully laughter. Instead, the sound of silence was common. Tears were a rare sound in these institutions. The children had simply stopped crying. They had learnt a painful lesson. Their tears did not bring change; their tears did not mean they would receive attention, food, a change of clothes, or a visit to the toilet. Crying was not the solution. There was no point in sobbing. The two under-trained, underpaid staff working fourteen hour shifts, just did not have the time to listen. It was pitiful. Bleak. Unclean. And an unsatisfactory way to raise children.

With a huge task ahead, I remained focussed and quickly settled into my new accommodation in Colombo. Home sweet home was a two-storey detached house near the coastline.

Throughout the country there were quiet underlying tensions between the Tamil and Sinhalese population. But on the surface both factions mixed. My landlord and cook were Tamil. My gardener Sinhalese. At work, the staff were a mixture of Tamil and Sinhalese. We all worked together. There was harmony in the office. It was important.

Time passed quickly in Sri Lanka, but the pace was as slow as the old Morris Minor cars and bullock carts that meandered through the streets. The heat and humidity were strong. Intense. The mosquitoes were also intense - intensely irritating! They accompanied me night and day with their high-pitched buzz. But aside from the unwelcome insect life I felt an immediate ease with the culture, people and pace. There was time to greet and meet the locals. I quickly made friends. English was the second language and the Brits were highly respected.

Little did I realise as I settled into my new way of life, that in just a few months time my Brit background would be used to its full advantage. Sri Lanka was on the brink of civil war. My white skin was going to help save a few souls.

When I began my job for *Save the Children* the last thing I predicted was that the gentle mild mannered Tamils and gracious quiet Sinhalese would be involved in a bloody, violent conflict that would leave thousands dead and thousands of homes destroyed.

Had I known what lay ahead, I would never have invited my daughter Kathryn and her friend Claire Skinner, to fly out for a visit. They were on their summer vacation from school and keen to do voluntary work abroad. I was keen for my daughter to experience another culture, country and climate. Looking at life on other sides of the globe I maintain is the best and only way to gain a well informed opinion of the world. If only George Bush had taken a good look around the world before he became president of the USA! It's hard to believe that he had never allegedly been outside of Texas and Washington before he tried to conquer parts of the planet as president.

Kathryn had more wanderlust than Mr Bush. I remember my joy as she arrived at the busy airport carrying a big suitcase and wearing a smile. We hugged. She seemed to have grown up another notch in the few months I had been away from home. Confidence and charm were part of her natural make-up.

"You missing Hemel Hempstead?" she asked smiling.

"Just the newspapers, football results and kippers," I joked.

It was true, I was not homesick. My working life was far too busy to allow me to yearn too much for friends, family or even kippers!

The girls quickly adapted to the Sri Lankan way of life and began working at a local orphanage. I was proud of my daughter. The feeling was mutual. She brought news of home. Graeme was enjoying university, Ann was busy with her job, my parents were fine and Chelsea were winning. It all seemed so far away from the heat, haze and easy pace of Colombo. But beneath the calm picture, all hell was about to break loose. Just days after Kathryn arrived, Colombo became a burning bloodbath. Violence, death, hatred and revenge

Chapter 17

spewed its ugly head on the city, as the worst side of humanity was unleashed.

The date was July 23, 1983, a bleak day that was later to be dubbed 'Black July'. It marked the start of a full-scale armed struggle between Tamil militants and the predominantly Sinhalese-dominated government. It began in the north of the country where it was reported that the Liberation Tigers of Tamil Eelam (LTTE) ambushed and publicly killed thirteen government soldiers as a brutal act of revenge against the soldiers who had raped Tamil women in their villages.

The bodies of the slaughtered government soldiers were insensitively and perhaps foolishly paraded in open coffins in Colombo. It was not a wise move. Tensions were high. The sight of death being marched through the streets pushed emotions to their limits. Two days later, on the day the soldiers were to be buried in Colombo, it was reported that some Sinhalese civilians who had gathered at the cemetery formed mobs. They started looting and burning Tamil properties and cars. Within hours, the once calm streets of the capital quickly became scenes of chaos and fear. Outside my home and office, gunshots were fired, and innocent men, women and children were fleeing for their lives. It was the first time in my life I had heard gunfire in conflict. The first time I had felt and smelt the panic of civil war. I remember standing quietly and helplessly by my desk, my eyes looking nervously out of the window, watching vehicles being torched while pedestrians fled through the streets in panic. My daughter and her friend had fled to my workplace, scared and excited by the chaos. I was more than relieved to see them.

Within a day the mobs were out in force. Eyewitnesses reported that groups of angered youths armed with cans of petrol were stopping passing motorists at critical street junctions. When the ethnic identity was known, they would set the vehicle alight. Other groups were moving through the city, looking for Tamil residents and using the official electoral list to find them. When a household was found, it would be torched. Smoke was rising above the city as murder, mayhem, death and destruction hung heavy in the air. At the office, we responded immediately to the crisis and concentrated on organising food distribution supplies for mothers and children.

In one of the emergency camps I visited to drop off supplies of milk powder, I struck up a friendship with a remarkable man – Tyrrell Cooray. He impressed me immediately with his calm, open hearted manner, his positive attitude and his concern for his people. He was very popular amongst the refugees in the camp. When Tyrrell had been asked to work at another camp, the refugees had petitioned that he must stay with them. Later, Tyrrell became my right arm advisor. We would meet both socially, sharing ideas and a stiff glass of arrack, a very pleasant Sri Lankan coconut whisky. My friendship with Tyrrell was going to last a lifetime.

Outside the refugee camps, chaos and death continued to sweep through the country but remarkably, I did not fear for my life. Tourists were in a state of panic and were trying to flee the country. Refugees from up-country were flocking into Colombo at an alarming rate, their houses burnt down and their lives in chaos.

My immediate response to the conflict was simply to ask myself - "What do we do in this situation? How can we help?" Save the Children was the only British charity in Sri Lanka at the time. I felt a huge sense of responsibility to set an example to my staff, and to the watching eyes of the world to do something positive for the innocent victims. I also felt a huge weight on my shoulders to get my daughter and her friend home. Ann had been calling almost daily. She was worried sick about Kathryn, Claire and me. No amount of reassuring could ease her troubled mind.

"I'll get them home, don't worry," I told her repeatedly.

It was easier said than done. Every day I made a gruelling drive to the airport hoping, praying and longing for a flight. Frustrating road checks made the one-hour journey long and tedious. Every day I had hope in my heart. But I lost count of the number of times we were sent home. Flights were rare. The airport was chaotic. Anxious tourists and ex-pats pleaded daily with airport staff to help them leave the country.

Persistently, I kept trying. I tried to remain optimistic.

Chapter 17

"We'll be fine dad," Kathryn would tell me. She was taking the unexpected adventure in her stride. On my umpteenth attempt to persuade airport staff to get my daughter home, luck, and a kind hearted captain of the KLM crew was on my side.

"I'll take them," he said. I wanted to throw my arms around him. Instead I hugged my daughter, said a quick farewell and watched them stride off to the awaiting aircraft. I was eternally grateful to KLM. The sense of relief was immense.

With Kathryn and Claire safely on their way back to Europe, I could concentrate on my increased workload, (now as Director), as well as my ever increasing concerns for my friends.

One of those colleagues, my young, loyal Tamil cleaner Manium, was on my mind night and day. He lived a 30-minute drive away from my home in an area that was under threat night and day. Families in his neighbourhood were running for their lives as the mobs swept through the area on a mission. Properties were being burnt to the ground. Families that remained in their homes faced going up in smoke. Without thought for my own life, I decided I would go in search of Manium and bring him and his family back to the safety of the empty rooms above the office.

Never had a half hour journey felt so long. Sitting behind the wheel of my jeep, I put my foot down, talked my way through roadblocks until I reached the familiar street where he lived. He saw me arrive. Standing by his front door, his young sister peeping out from behind him, his face broke into a relieved half smile. He knew why I had come. Clutching four carrier bags full of his possessions he instructed his mum and sister to swiftly follow him to my vehicle.

"Get in the back and lay on the floor," I quietly instructed. "Cover yourselves with the blankets."

He did as he was told. Crouching beneath a heavy blanket with his family by his side, they lay in the back of the vehicle, their bodies turned to statues. Apart from their beating hearts, there was no other movement. I was sweating. Not from the heat but from fear. If my concealed passengers were discovered, our vehicle might be torched. We could all go up in smoke. I had already received threatening phone calls from both sides of the struggle. Their tone was menacing. Alarming. Worrying.

"We know where you are, we know who you are," the sinister voices down the phone would frequently tell me. I dreaded the phone ringing.

Concentrating hard on the road ahead, I pushed on through the streets, confidently trying to use my white skin and my charity status to get us through roadblocks along the way.

"I'm working for *Save the Children*," I told the agitated mob members as they paced around my vehicle. Minutes from home, watchful eyes spotted the hidden passengers in the back. Stones were hurled angrily at the jeep. My heart leapt into my mouth. Adrenalin kicked in, but I tried to remain calm. Keeping my foot down and my hand on the horn to make as much noise as possible, we crawled through the streets while the angered mob members beat their fists on the side of the vehicle.

"Nearly there," I reassured my petrified passengers and myself. "Stay under the blankets." Turning several street corners, we moved away from the stoning and the green green grass of home became closer. Safety was in my grasp.

Sighing with relief, I parked the jeep outside my office headquarters and swiftly moved the Tamil family into a spare room. They were clearly shaken by the journey. The old lady had fear in her eyes. The sister was gently sobbing in her mother's arms. Manium thanked me endlessly.

That night I had a restless evening of interrupted sleep. I rewound the events of the day in my mind. Thankfully, Manium and his family were relatively safe under the watchful eye of our Sinhalese security guard VJ. It could have been a very different story. I had tasted danger. Felt real fear but despite putting my life and others on the line, I was at ease with my actions. I may have taken a risk, but it was the right decision. To have turned my back and done nothing to help Manium and his family would have haunted me. To do something, however big or small, is always the best option.

Days later, I faced an even greater risk. My landlady was Tamil. She lived in the back of my house. Local Tamils were being sought out by means of the electoral register. Homes

Chapter 17

were being burnt. Innocent people were being targeted. The mobs were coming our way. Fear was in the air and in the veins of my landlady.

"Can you help us," she begged. "Please can you help us," she repeated. Turning my back was not an option. We hatched a plan and hoped it would work. Standing tall beneath a night sky, I placed myself defiantly by the gate of our home and waited, waited, waited for the mob to arrive. All I could hope was that my white face would save my skin, and everyone else's. It was a long night. I had hours to think. Hours to endure the fear and reality of conflict. But in my moment of crisis, I learnt so much. When faced with the loss of your home, your family or having to flee for your life, material possessions go out the window. What matters in the end is far simpler. I had, in my pockets, everything I needed . . . my passport, some money, two oranges and four bananas. The grandfather clock that I'd grown fond of in my Sri Lankan home lost its importance. I loved that clock. I loved the way it stood as proud as a soldier on parade. I loved the comforting sound of its strong, methodical tick and heavy swinging pendulum. But I was prepared to leave it behind.

Pieces of fruit and the need to eat and know where your next meal is coming from are far more crucial than a huge timepiece. It was an interesting exercise but one I wished I had not endured. I had been fairly naïve about war when I had arrived in Sri Lanka. I was learning lessons fast.

In the early hours of the morning, I watched in horror as an angry mob moved down the street. Behind them, homes were blazing. Flames flickered against the dark sky. Smoke poured towards the heavens. I shuffled nervously as the mob moved closer. And closer. One of them strode towards me and stood within inches of my face. He was a young man. He was on a mission and moved purposefully, without showing an ounce of fear or hesitation. For that brief moment in time, I could do nothing but hope and pray. What was going on in this young man's mind? Was I going to become his next victim? Would he burn my home? What was his next move? Eyeballing me and looking me up and down, I kept my head high. My heart pounded, beating hard against my chest. Miraculously, we were all spared. I am here today to pass this story on to my grandchildren. Unbelievably, our home was saved by a parked car on the opposite side of the road. That lump of metal was the perfect distraction that took the mob away from me. That magnificent motor became the priority of the approaching mob. They wanted the car more than they wanted my Tamil landlady, her family, her house and me.

Smashing the windows of the vehicle, they shouted triumphantly, started the engine, and drove off victoriously down the street. For a moment my feet remained rooted to the ground and I inhaled a deep lungful of the warm evening air.

In the days and weeks that followed, the country remained in chaos. Several cities throughout Sri Lanka experienced similar unrest. Curfews were in place. Medical supplies were unavailable. Misery and suffering was under my nose. I visited refugee camps that had been set up to accommodate the thousands of civilians that had fled for their lives. It was a sight I will not forget. Endless canvas makeshift homes stood side by side. Living conditions were harsh. With little or almost nothing to do for days, weeks, months on end, boredom, crime and sexual abuse became prevalent. Children looked for parents, and death was mourned daily. Food was in short supply. And distribution of basic needs of flour, bread, rice and sugar began. *Save the Children* responded to the crisis, working round the clock to try and make life just a little bit better for those in need.

In the cities, the food shortages forced civilians to queue for almost everything edible. I frequently joined the bread queue. In the heat of the morning, I stood in a snake like line of patient people who would wait for more than ninety minutes for a small loaf. Conditions in the city were harsh. Tense. Although calm had been restored, and curfews were ceased, the clean up and resettlement of thousands of refugees was going to be an enormous task.

Chris Patten, (now Lord Patten of Barnes), the then Overseas Development Minister arrived in Sri Lanka in 1985. I accompanied him to some of the worst affected areas. He was well informed, sensitive and keen to see for himself what was happening on the ground. I was more than keen to show him. Following his visit, Mrs Thatcher responded to the crisis on a mission to give aid to Sri Lanka. She wanted to be seen by the British, and the world to be doing the right thing. She arrived in the country, cameras watching her every move. She addressed the Sri Lankan government. She shook my hand. Most importantly, she announced that she would be putting her hand in her governmental pocket. We were the only British agency in the country. A huge grant would be coming our way. Five million pounds worth of aid over three years. Every penny was needed. And what's more, Mrs Thatcher agreed that we could determine where the money would be spent. I shared a celebratory beer or two with my work colleagues following this good news. Swiftly, we planned where the money would be placed and made sure it would not spend months, sitting in the bank.

We introduced three hundred crucial Supplementary Feeding Programmes up and down the country. They were run by mothers. But more funding was needed for long-term aid. Lactating mothers, and mums and young children were a priority. Our aim was to distribute powdered milk and provide permanent facilities for these needy women and children.

A speedy response to any worldly natural crisis or war is crucial. Aid often pours into charities following disasters, but often sits unspent for far too long or alternatively does not look at long term need.

Every ten months I left the heat and haze behind and returned to Hemel Hempstead to catch up with the family and friends. Ann would meet me from the airport, a welcoming smile on her face, and drive me home. On that thirty-minute journey I would try to adjust quickly to the sights and sounds of the UK. Cows grazing, traffic roaring, and bleak winter weather had been absent from my life in Sri Lanka. So had kippers. I didn't miss the cold weather but I did miss the taste of fresh kippers gently cooked and served up for supper or breakfast. Ann always made sure she filled the fridge with my favourite foods when I came home.

The phone never stopped ringing during my UK visits. "How

are you Bob?" "Come and see us?" was the familiar request.

My parents, the children and time with Ann were of course a priority. I tried to keep up with family, friends and neighbours but to visit them all was an impossible task. The solution was simple. A homecoming party was usually arranged. Everyone was invited. And everyone came.

Our parties were huge occasions. We often turned them into talent contests. Guests would come with guitars, poems and songs to sing or jokes to tell. Creating a mini stage in the back garden or living room we would gather round and watch the show. Ann needed little excuse to sing. Nor did I. Blacking up my face I would pull on some white gloves and turn myself into Al Jolson. It was not the first time I'd changed the colour of my skin and belted out the very same songs. My debut as Al Jolson had been staged in the Crypt at St Martins-in-the-Fields church in London on Christmas day when I was just 23 years old. I had volunteered to help feed the homeless a festive meal. But I went one notch further than just handing out plates of turkey. I joined in with the impromptu cabaret that took place after dessert.

"Climb upon my knee sonny boy," was my favourite. Now, decades later in Hemel Hempstead, I was belting out the same song. Thankfully I was still fit enough to sink down onto one knee Al Jolson style. Getting up again, after a few drinks was not so easy.

If I wasn't impersonating Al Jolson, I'd turn my hand to a spot of Tommy Cooper style magic. I was about as good at magic as I had been at ballroom dancing in my teens. But I did my best to impress my guests. By the end of the party, I could at least boast that I had helped make the drink and food disappear. A good time was had "just like that" by all.

Jumping continents became a way of life. It suited me, and Ann coped well with my absences, getting her teeth stuck into her job, friends and family. But in late 1985, my return trip to the UK was not such a joyful occasion. When I least expected it, I had received some chilling news in Sri Lanka. My dad was on the other end of the phone. His voice was breaking with emotion.

Chapter 17

"Your mum has just died," he told me. Burying my head in my hands, I could barely believe his words. My dear, kind, gentle mother was dead and I had not been there to see her in her last moments of life. My guilt was overwhelming. I flew home immediately, my heart broken. If only I had seen mum before she passed away. I could not have saved her, she died of pneumonia. But I could have at least held her hand one last time, stroked her hair, and let her know just how much she meant to me.

It had been mum's request that we scatter her ashes in Hemel Hempstead's Rose Garden. It was a place she loved to visit. I often remember her, as sweet as the flowers, walking through the garden, or walking beside me as a child, or standing in the Balham kitchen, serving up a bowl of broth. Fond memories.

On one of my many flights back to Colombo airport, I struck up conversation with a fellow passenger in the next seat. He was Dutch. He wanted to chat. So our idle chitchat began. Once we had covered the weather in England, the in-flight food and his country, our idle chatter very quickly moved into deeper waters. This man wanted to tell me about his job. I wished he hadn't.

"I'm selling arms in Sri Lanka," he told me while sipping his in-flight whisky.

"Arms?" I questioned, horrified.

"Yes, that's right," he continued without an inch of remorse. "Arms to both sides and I hope this war will continue as long as possible."

His words hit me hard. I was immediately reminded of Mitch Allan's words on war in his memorable book ' Tuesdays with Morrie' - "You have a few people with everything and a military to keep the poor ones from rising up and stealing it."

This man was helping fuel the military. If I could have pressed a James Bond style eject button and have him blasted into space, I would have done. Instead he continued to tell me more about his unsavoury work. Shoulder to shoulder in our cramped seats, I felt increasingly uncomfortable beside this man. His job helped create blood, tears and suffering. My job involved clearing it all up. It made my skin crawl being in his presence.

I could not endure the next eight hours beside him. There was no eject button and a mid flight brawl would not have gone down well with the other passengers. Instead I chose to have myself removed as far away from Mr Bomb Seller as possible.

"I'd like to move seats," I asked the stewardess. " As soon as possible."

Thankfully, my request was granted. The remaining hours of my journey were spent a comfortable distance from my new enemy.

Back in Colombo, the capital was slowly recovering from civil war. I could no longer smell the fear. People were trying to rebuild their lives but the refugee camps remained full to bursting point. *Save the Children* continued to restore, rebuild and re-house those in need. I met and talked to people from all sides of the conflict. I saw mothers mourning their dead children, grandparents, silently accepting their homelessness and bewildered youngsters scratching around refugee camps trying to come to terms with horrors they had witnessed. I also came face to face with a potential suicide bomber. I was on one of my many journeys across the country, taking supplies to different regions when I experienced this unusual encounter. My vehicle had been stopped on the road by a group of khaki dressed young men. They were all Tamil Tigers, all committed to their cause. One of them walked forward. Around his neck he carried a small capsule. It contained cyanide, cyanide that he would readily swallow to end his own life. His portion of poison showed he was ready to die for his cause. We exchanged a few words. I wanted to understand his impassioned mind. I wanted him to understand my way of thinking. There was no time for a debate.

"Why?" was my simple question. I knew he could not be converted. He believed death for his cause was better than life itself and would bring glory in the after-life. I believed there had to be another way forward. Our brief encounter was chilling. How would a young man with a whole life ahead of him be so willing to swallow his cyanide and lie down and die, rather than be taken prisoner? It is a thought that has run through my mind in the past few years since suicide bombing has spilled over onto our shores. It seems a hopeless situation. No threatened consequences will act as a deterrent.

Writing letters to Ann and the children, I edited out the more worrying side of my life in Sri Lanka. 'Dear Ann, I have just met a suicide bomber' would not have been the words she wanted to receive. Or 'Dear Ann our vehicle narrowly escaped falling off the mountainside after a boulder was rolled in its path,' may have prompted a few premature grey hairs on her head. Instead, I told her about the sweeter side of life overseas. I told her that I was active in using sport to breakdown barriers. I had founded a cricket team, the Ceylon Cavaliers. Team members were Tamil and Sinhalese as well as Brits, Australians and New Zealanders. Tamils and Sinhalese were also part of the national rugby squad that I was coaching. Aside from sport, I also cheerily wrote about my Scottish Dancing achievements. "I'm in the B team Ann," I boasted. "We will be dancing at the St Andrews Ball." It sounded grand. It made me look like I had been born to dance the Highland jig. In reality the B team was nothing to write home about. There were so few Scottish dancers in Sri Lanka, that as long as you could stand on two feet, you automatically gained entry into team B.

When I wasn't dancing I was enjoying Hash, (not the smoking variety), but the fifty runners that met once a week and jogged, sprinted, limped or strolled for an hourly cross country paper chase. Physical exercise was good for me. Lined up in my white shorts and running shoes, I'd take deep breaths of the heavy heat and get ready for the off.

I ran alongside expats, locals and fellow workers and completed a total of 169 runs during my time in Sri Lanka. I was keen. But far slower than everyone else. As they sprinted towards the paddy fields avoiding snakes along the way, I'd drop so far back that nobody would have noticed if I disappeared to the nearest bar. My pace was always more tortoise than hare speed. I was clearly not the fittest Brit abroad. 'Plodder', was my nickname. It was a fitting title. Plodding was my speciality and a name that stuck during my time in Sri Lanka. Only when I gained my PhD in Social Policy and Public Administration did my nickname change. I simply became 'Dr Plod.'

Looking back, my time in Sri Lanka was one of the best and most rewarding periods of my life. My initial two-year contract stretched, stretched, stretched into an eight-year period of work. I did my best for the people of Sri Lanka. They had also given so much to me. They became my life. Their names and faces, devotion and loyalty remain etched in my memory and heart. My wonderful secretaries Nalini, Marnel and Rangi always gave 110%. My work colleagues Leslie, Shan and Tyrrell did the same.

"The most important appointments are your cook and driver," Leslie had advised. They were words of wisdom. Richard was capable and creative in the kitchen. I thought of him as my very own master chef. Even Jamie Oliver would have been impressed. Thiru was extremely skilled on the road. He was a fantastic driver who got me in and out of traffic and trouble on the road. In very different ways they both safeguarded my life. As well as being supported by my staff, my family in England were also very strong pillars in my life. Ann and the children visited when they could and kept the home fire burning in Hemel Hempstead. They were always there for me and were in particularly high spirits when I found out that I had been awarded the MBE for my work during the civil war. Initially I was reluctant to accept it.

"It's my staff that deserve the award." I explained to the British High Commissioner who had recommended me. "It's my staff that have done so much."

After much thought and discussion, I accepted my MBE only on the basis it was given to my staff members as well as myself. The work team were delighted for me.

"MBE? Does that mean My Bloody Efforts? " I joked with work colleagues behind the scenes. "Surely I should have been awarded the OBE instead."

"And why's that?" they asked curiously.

"OBE, stands for the Other Buggers Efforts." I explained, laughing.

Jokes aside, it was the truth. Without my team, which had grown from 30 to 300 committed workers, I would have achieved very little during my time in Sri Lanka. With them behind me, everything was possible.

Carrying each and every one of them in my heart, I attended my appointment with HRH Queen Elizabeth to receive the award at Buckingham Palace. Ann, Graeme and Kathryn could accompany me for the occasion. I polished my shoes, wore my best tartan kilt, straightened my sporan and practiced a smile.

Graeme, me and Kathryn, at Buckingham Palace 1990

Entering the palace was special. We were warmly greeted. Handshakes began. With heads held high we followed our host to a very grand hall. My eyes scanned my surroundings. I'd gone from the streets of Balham to Buckingham Palace and felt determined to make the most of every second. Kathryn, Graeme and Ann felt the same. We raised our eyebrows repeatedly, equally impressed by every inch of the decor. When my moment came to meet the Queen I was aglow with pride. She smiled delicately. Unrushed, we had a brief chat. Not about the weather or the corgis. Her Majesty was well briefed and prepared to ask me about my time in Sri Lanka.

"Its' a wonderful country," I told her. "But the war has tainted it." She nodded and continued to talk. I was impressed. So were my family as they watched from the sidelines. I felt bigger than my size eleven-polished footwear. I'm not usually one for ceremonies, but this MBE was special. It meant a lot. Standing tall in Buckingham Palace, I thought of all my loyal staff in Sri Lanka and most of all I thought of my three members of staff who never came home. They had died as a result of the internal conflict in the civil war. They were on my mind when I received my award. I was most certainly receiving the award for them as well.

Returning to Sri Lanka, I took the impressive, shiny medal back with me. It was proudly placed in a frame and hung on the wall near my desk. It has remained there to this day.

Making the decision to leave Sri Lanka was difficult. But all chapters in life must come to a close in order for the next one to begin. The UK was on my mind and calling me back to its shores. My dad was unwell, my father-in-law was also in poor health. It was time to go home and take on the new job as Regional Director for Asia. Commuting to London from my home sweet home in Hemel Hempstead, I could keep a watchful eye on my dad and father in law. But saying farewell to so many good friends, and all the familiar places was an emotional wrench. Several leaving parties were arranged, several glasses of arrack were sunk, and I received so many presents that my luggage was bursting at the seams. Emotionally I was in pieces.

"We won't forget you," said my friends at the airport. And nor would I ever forget them. Sri Lanka and its people had touched me deeply. As my plane bound for England nudged its way into the clouds, I buried my head in a book and swallowed back my tears. A grown man crying is not a pleasant sight. My only comfort was that I could finally say goodbye to the irritating mosquitoes that pestered me night and day with

Chapter 17

their incessant high-pitched buzzing. As the saying goes...
if you think small is beautiful, try sleeping with a mosquito.
Goodbye Sri Lanka. Goodbye mosquito nights.

18

Around the World in Heat and Haze

Floods in Bangladesh, bloodshed in Burma, poverty in Pakistan and child prostitution in the Philippines and India. I witnessed it all, jumping from one country to the next as the *Save the Children* Regional Director for Asia. Powerful stories of survival, horror and human kindness unfolded. I would never be the same again. Materialism and greed became my enemy when I returned to the UK.

He was at least seventy years old and had deep lines etched on his sun-baked skin. He was homeless and had nothing left of his former life except the clothes he stood up in and a memory of what used to be. His humble corrugated iron roofed home and all his possessions had been swept away in a torrent of water when the riverbeds burst in Bangladesh in 1991. His home had been located on low ground. It did not stand a chance of remaining upright. I tried to place myself in his shoes. Just how would it feel to find that my Hemel Hempstead home and all its contents had floated off in a river of fast flowing water never to be seen again? This dear old man was just one of the many thousands of people who needed help following the Bangladesh flooding. It was the fifth time he had lost his house in the floods. And I was reminded of this scene when the July 2007 floods devastated areas of the UK.

Save the Children had responded to the Bangladesh disaster and flown out a team of medical staff and advisors. They were working round the clock, moving the homeless to temporary emergency shelter, trying to identify need and trying to encourage the homeless to be re-housed in less disaster prone locations. The old man was on my long list of people to advise. His family had requested I paid him a visit.

"Will you let us move you to higher ground?" I asked him, with the help of an interpreter. I tried to explain the reasons why this made sense. Bangladesh had a history of natural flooding disasters. If we rebuilt the old mans home in the same low ground location, it would be vulnerable in the future. The old man listened carefully. But shaking his head defiantly as I spoke, he would not be talked into anything.

"I have lived here all my life," he explained. "My parents lived here before me. My ancestors are part of this land," he gently stated. And as he talked he looked around the boggy ground that had once been his home. It was his place. It contained precious memories, it had been the home he knew and loved, the place where he had run as a child, and the familiar land where his grandchildren had followed in his footsteps. He knew every tree and bush. He knew the soil, the view and everyone around him.

I knew he would never budge and nor should I try to change his mind. He had raised his four children here. His entire life and peace of mind was attached to this flooded location. I had to respect his needs to return to his old homestead. Moving to higher ground in his mind was not an acceptable option. His defiance and determination touched me deeply.

All over Bangladesh, the homeless were struggling to come to terms with their individual losses. I waded through floodwaters in different areas, trying to reach the people that needed help. Bangladesh was renowned for flooding. Every few years, nature cuts a cruel path through Bangladesh, destroying homes, lives, and livelihoods. And every few years the world responds to help the victims of disaster.

At the time of these Bangladesh floods, I had been working for *Save the Children* as Regional Director. Behind me had been a long, intense tour of South East Asia visiting fourteen countries. My job as Regional Director, had involved monitoring the work of the charity, supporting the staff located in the UK and locally, discussing budgets, and recruiting staff in the UK for work around the globe. India, Pakistan, Nepal, Cambodia, Tibet, China, Bhutan, Vietnam and the Philippines were just a few of the countries stamped in my passport. Many of them shared similar problems; all of them had problems of their own. I respected the rhythm, religion and culture of each country and, from mistakes made, learnt vital lessons along the way.

In Bangladesh, hundreds of thousands of water purifying tablets were purchased following the floods. We believed the people would need them, as clean water would keep sickness at bay. But not one of those white tablets was issued. The local people drank the water and did not become sick. Their systems were strong and had grown used to the contaminated water.

My time as regional director was a huge lesson in my life. I was walking into the face of disaster, poverty, conflict, hunger and hopelessness. But I felt privileged and frequently humbled by my experiences. I can still remember the faces of the old, the sick, the young and the newborn. I saw tears of desperation, and tears of jubilation. I witnessed sights that I wished I could erase from my mind. But as the saying goes – what doesn't kill you makes you stronger.

On a flight from Calcutta (now Kolkata) to Thimphu in Bhutan, a flying experience with DRUK airlines tested this theory 150%. Hair raising was an understatement. I was one of three passengers. We were all weighed prior to departure and seated accordingly to balance the load. In-flight food was a biscuit and a glass of water. A stiff whisky and a sedative would have been more appropriate. We were going to be flying right through the mountains of the Himalayas. As we took off I closed my eyes and thought of England. To the left and right of me, peaks touched the tops of clouds and all I could do was hope that visibility remained clear and the pilot didn't stray from the central path. The scenery was spectacular but, given the choice I would have opted to view the Himalayas on a tv screen. This short flight was a test of my nerves. Never have I been so pleased to see Paro runway. I survived, but I'm not sure if I was stronger for it.

Chapter 18

During a visit to Burma (now renamed Myanmar), my trip coincided with an uprising by Buddhist priests and students against the military dictatorship. It was a horrifying, terrifying time of bloodshed. Every day in the capital city of Rangoon, casualties of all ages, were carried into the Embassy where I was staying. They had been attacked, maimed or injured for protesting against the brutal military regime. Casualties and death were common.

Fear and panic were in the air. The locals, tourists and the overseas workforce were more than anxious. Trying to leave the country was dangerous. I stayed for one, long week. My job was frustrating. I had gone with the intention of starting a training programme for staff in residential care. There was an urgent need for this programme to be implemented. But to make that happen meant a huge battle to break down the hostility towards foreigners. I hit several bureaucratic brick walls. The country and its people needed help. But the controlling powers just didn't want to take it. You can't win them all. I struggled to accept that.

I remember leaving for the airport, a flag on my chauffeur driven car to indicate I was working for *Save the Children*. Along the way, lining the streets, were soldiers with rifles. Guns were pointing in our direction, tracing our movement. All it would take was one finger on the trigger to open fire. I truly believed that at any moment, we would be the next targets, the next casualty, the next horror report. There was nothing I could do but hope and pray that I wasn't another statistic in this bloody conflict. Running the gauntlet, I reached the airport, my heart thumping through my chest. I tried to relax. I bought a drink and a newspaper. But the graphic powerful photo on the front page sickened, saddened and haunted me to this day.

The disturbing image that turned my head and stomach was of an old man captured moments before his death. The man had been forced down onto his knees, his hands clasped together, fear stamped on his face. He was staring at the ground, begging for his life while a soldier stands above him ready to pull the trigger. Moments later, that helpless old man was cold-heartedly shot dead. He was a victim of the oppressive regime. He had not committed a crime. He was used as a scapegoat. His death was to demonstrate to the local people that the army of soldiers who had been shrewdly brought in from outside the capital, had no identity and feeling towards those around them. Old, young, men and women would have the same fate if they joined the uprising.

Back in the UK, in the comfort of my home, or walking the streets of my local town, my experiences in Myanmar and beyond ran through my veins. On one side of the world men, women and children were starving or fighting for survival. On the other, they were shopping and trying to lose weight. I had a foot on both sides of the globe. Caring for the world and its people was part of my character and as a Quaker, it was what I wholeheartedly believed in. Naïvely, when I returned to England, I expected almost everyone who crossed my path to have similar concerns. I was wrong. Although I met numerous extremely kind and giving souls, there were many others who chose to be blind to the world around them. Their cold hearts and materialistic minds sometimes bothered me. Selfishness and excessive self-indulgence were hard to accept and sometimes I struggled when I stepped from one world to another.

Ahead of me a new chapter was about to begin. I had made the difficult decision to leave *Save the Children* charity. Although I was based in London, so much of my work with them had been overseas. I was keen to spend less time jumping on and off planes and spend more time in the UK with my family. I returned to the Probation Service in London They had headhunted me. They were short of experienced staff and were keen that I worked with their more difficult clients in the Kings Cross area of London. Spending my working day in the drugs centre of London would be a challenge. I accepted the job on the condition that I would take short-term assignments for *Save the Children* to set up programmes for street children in Ghana, then to advise the Ministry of Justice in Malawi on implementing Community Service Orders as an alternative to custodial sentences. But little did I realise that

Chapter 18

Save the Children were soon going to be tapping me on the shoulder again to become their Tracing Consultant in war torn countries. I would soon be packing my bag and flying into the face of death, despair and desperation in Liberia, Sierra Leone and Rwanda.

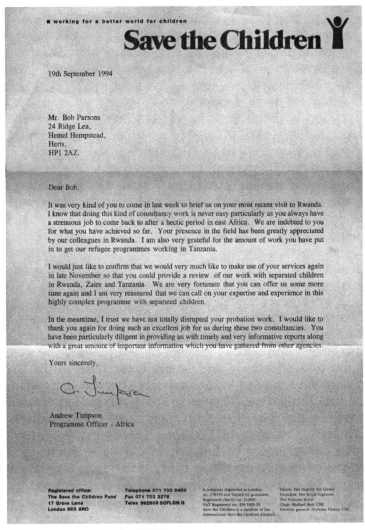

A letter from Save the Children

19

Lost Children

Rwanda, 1994. I arrived, via Kampala in Uganda on a freight flight. Beside me were 25,000 empty body bags. The genocide was not yet over. It was a chilling one-month visit that would shape my future.

As far as the eye could see there were tents. Blue United Nations tents. Inside the plastic temporary shelters were children, mothers, fathers and grandparents huddled together, communally sharing their grief, shock and nightmares. They were the survivors. They had fled to the safety of the refugee camps in neighbouring countries. Behind them, in villages throughout Rwanda were the innocent victims that had been massacred by machetes, killed by gunfire or burnt alive. The carnage was still going on. It was too close for comfort.

On my first night in Kigali, the house in which I was staying had come under gunfire. Huddled on the floor, beneath a window, random shots from the darkness of the night shattered the windows. I was scared. Who wouldn't be? Thankfully, the morning arrived, and I kept breathing.

I had arrived on a short-term contract with *Save the Children* to set up a child-tracing programme. In this terrible genocide, thousands upon thousands of people had been forced to run for their lives. In panic and desperation, many had run in different directions to family members. 100,000 children were reported missing or lost from their families. That's a shocking statistic. Imagine filling the new Wembley Stadium with children. And every one of those kids being lost, bewildered

Chapter 19

individuals, desperately trying to find their parents. This was the reality before my eyes. Children had been parted from their mothers; husbands had been forced to flee from their wives, brothers, and sisters. It was harrowing and heartbreaking.

As always, I kept my emotions at bay and concentrated on my work. In a crisis, I would be no good to anyone if I fell to my knees, overwhelmed by the sight, sounds and smell of conflict, or disaster.

My new home was in the refugee camp just over the border in Tanzania. I worked in a blue United Nations tent. I slept in one. Facilities were basic. Around me was a community of 76,000 refugees all sleeping in tents. I was fortunate to have a sleeping bag.

A long first night stretched ahead. Sleep was light. Broken. I was woken at 4.30 am by the sound of chopping wood, a baby crying and dogs barking. I longed for daylight to arrive. In the air was an indefinable stench – a combination of burning wood, urine and decay.

As the sun rose, I quickly dressed, doused my face from a bucket of murky water kindly left outside the tent by my neighbour. The camp was busy. People were washing and drying their clothes, preparing fires, joining long queues for rations, beating maize and setting off to collect wood. There was a strange sense of order as each member of the tented household knew his or her task. A girl around six years old assumed the maternal role, looking after her three naked younger siblings cladding them in shoddy vests, knickers or pants. I was ready for my working day. The task facing us was enormous.

We worked all hours. With the help of a local interpreter, and with paper, pens, Kodak cameras and films, I would listen carefully as countless nightmare stories unfolded.

The very first youngster I interviewed was Emmarend Munera, a Rwandan Hutu refugee. He was eight. He looked about fourteen. He came from the Muranuli Commune in Bunamba from a family consisting of mother, father, and nine brothers and sisters. An unknown group attacked his home. He was the sole survivor. He faked being dead for eight hours, lying next to members of his dead family until the attackers left. He received machete wounds on the back of his head, lost teeth and suffered considerable loss of blood. He walked for ten days living rough and begging for food to reach the camp. He was one of the many lost, lonely, frightened, traumatised children who made their way to my *Save the Children* tent, hoping and praying we could help them trace their families. Their eyes, hollowed, lifeless and almost turned to stone, said it all. Their young minds were haunted by what they had witnessed. Their young hearts were heavy with burden, worry and fear.

Young Rwandan refugees

Every child was important. Every child mattered. And, if possible every child would have a file made on them, a file that contained the details of where they lived, and who was in their family. We photographed them all individually and placed each sad, pathetic snapshot on a huge board outside our tent.

Face after face lined the board. It was a giant wall of grief.

Chapter 19

But it was also a wall of hope. Around the camp the displaced families that arrived were told to report to the *Save the Children* tent if their child was missing.

And they came in their hundreds and thousands. Silently, slowly, with hope running through their veins that they may just find a photo of their beloved lost youngster displayed on the board of missing children.

To reunite one child to the bosom of their mother means everything. Thankfully, there were many of these emotional, overwhelming moments. I remember witnessing one of those powerful reunions. First came the smiles, and then came the sobbing as desperate limbs clung onto other desperate limbs, frightened to let go again. I saw countless children who were lost, alone, and shell-shocked. One child who made his way to camp was so traumatised that he would not speak. He was around eleven years old. No amount of gentle communication would coax him into talking. His eyes were glazed, his mouth frozen. He stared at me, locked in his own private nightmare.

I slept lightly at the end of each day, exhausted by the work but determined to do as much as possible to help the innocent victims. At night in the camp, thousands of people would be closing their eyes to try and escape the horrors that ran through their minds. In the hillside, around the camp, gunshot fire continued as the bloody battle raged on.

It was a senseless conflict. Tutsis and Hutus were at war. Before the genocide they had been friends. They had worked together, lived together, and married each other. Now they were firm enemies who would savagely murder, maim and massacre each other. I was not interested in who was to blame, or who started the genocide. I was there to do a job and not judge or take sides.

We took our tracing programme and our photos to hospitals and prisons, spread the word and our wings as far as possible. Sometimes we would come across abandoned babies, too young to tell us where they came from, but hopefully too young to remember the massacre that may have taken place in their village, or the mothers that had held them to their breast.

On one of my many wanderings throughout Kigali, I came

across a woman who was to change my life and shape my future. Her name was Maisie. She was around fifty years old and illiterate. Her smile was gentle and welcoming. Her story was heart wrenching.

Maisie had lost every one of her family members. Her sons, daughter, grandchildren and husband had been wiped out before her eyes. But this woman did not lie down and let her own spirit die. Instead, she took in two orphaned children and gave them the love and security they needed.

Within a week of looking after the two young orphans, several more children had been brought to her door. She opened that door. She opened her heart and took them in. Every day, more children would arrive hungry for love and security. She never turned them away.

When I visited she had fifty youngsters under her wing. They slept together in one room, huddled under empty grain sacks on the bare floor, a huge hungry litter of orphaned pitiful souls. Yet, in her care they had a roof over their head, a meal a day, the security of a home, and the love of her huge heart that must have been grieving for her own children and grandchildren.

Without the backing or funding of charity she had set up her own 'orphanage'. Maisie simply felt a need to do something. Every day was a struggle for this middle-aged mother but she smiled defiantly as she ran around after her flock. She was an inspiration, an example of the strength of the human spirit.

Putting my hand in my pocket, I handed over some of my own money. But I wanted to do more to help this great woman. She would not leave my thoughts. So that evening, I appealed to several large UK charities to support her and her huge extended family. I asked them for funds. I put her case forward. "Please," I added. "She needs funding."

They all refused. She was turned down simply because she was not registered as a charity or an organisation. It was not what I wanted to hear. On that hot July evening, in 1994, I lost faith in larger charities. Their strict policies did not give them room to recognize the individuals that need help in an emergency situation or crisis. They could only help the larger registered organisations and had to turn their backs on amazing people like Maisie. Sadly, despite her desperate need, she and many others slipped through the big charity net.

Disillusioned, disheartened, I could not get this woman out of my mind. There were so many more like Maisie scattered throughout Rwanda and the world. Who was there to help them in their time of need? With that thought in mind, when my contract was over, and I left Rwanda and its tracing programme in motion, I did not forget my experiences. Maisie remained firmly in my thoughts. I could not turn my back on her. Instead I eventually found a small charity that would give her support and funding. We kept in contact. Proudly she built an extension on her home to house all the waifs and strays.

I felt satisfied she had the help she deserved. But Maisie never left my thoughts. She had planted a seed in me. A seed that was destined to grow. A seed that was going to bring hope to those that needed a helping hand in life. Just around the corner of my own life, I was going to be starting a small charity for children – a charity that would support small projects like Maisie's. It wasn't something I had planned or dreamt about in my life. But it was going to happen. It was meant to happen.

20

Farewell Dad

It was his last ride. A slow gentle meander through the streets he had known and loved. I smiled gently for my father as his flower-laden coffin and the funeral cortege trailed past his favourite three places in life . . . his beloved Wimbledon Football Club, the greyhound track and his local pub - The Grove. He would have loved his final journey.

1 991, was the last year of my dad's life. I had settled back into the UK and was working hard for the probation service. My in-laws had passed on and I was keeping a close eye on my father. His health had been slowly fading for many months. We had seen the signs. Dad was becoming forgetful. Muddled. Confused. We had tried to retain his independence for as long as possible. For the first time in his life, I had a phone installed in his home. A daily chat down the line, I believed would be good for my father. I was wrong. For dad, a ringing phone was an event of the day and in his mind always meant an emergency. Every time he answered my daily call he was close to panic procedures. "What's the matter? What's happening? You all right? What's going on?" he would anxiously ask. It didn't matter how many times I told him I was just ringing to say "hi" the same emergency response kicked in the following day.

Dad also started making daily visits to the Post Office. In his hand was his pension book. Every day he demanded his pension. Every day they turned him away. He didn't mind. He simply returned with the same request 24 hours later.

Chapter 20

Graeme moved in with him for six months. It was a temporary reprieve. Graeme helped dad cook, clean, and cope with life. He gave his time and patience, but dad needed round the clock care. I had to accept that the bold, independent father I had once known was now struggling with age and dementia.

Alzheimer's was diagnosed. It wasn't a surprise. But the symptoms of this common condition were painful to witness. Nobody likes to see a loved one deteriorate. Dad's mind and body had always been active. He had been a hard worker all his life and taken pride in his independence. Even when mum had died, dad adjusted and coped remarkably well. He had cooked his own meals, kept a tidy clean house, a tidy mind and a sharp sense of humour. One by one, these strong characteristics collapsed.

Three generations of Parsons at dads 70th birthday celebrations.

Reluctantly, I made the decision to move dad into St George's Hospital in Tooting. It had a care home for the elderly. I packed his clothes into a small case and with my heart heavy, I led dad away from the comforts of his first floor flat. It was an awful moment. I knew he would never return to his comfy chair that sat a few feet away from the television. Nor would he be back in his own bed, or pottering around the kitchen. Dad had his own room at St George's but it wouldn't have mattered if he had an en-suite luxury room with a view, he just did not want to be there. Twice a week I would visit dad. Pulling up a chair, I'd sit beside his bed. For an hour, I'd talk and he would listen. I wasn't sure if he was digesting my words. He rarely responded. I'd tell him about his grandchildren, the weather, and then I would turn the clocks back and we'd reminisce on his brothers, the war, and his life.

At the end of my visit, I'd wrap my arms round dad's frail frame and we'd hug goodbye. Then, pausing beside the door, I would wave to him while he remained hunched and confused by his bed. I knew he wanted to accompany me home. He didn't say that in words or gestures. He didn't have to. That much I knew.

It broke my heart to walk away from dad. Always he would shuffle over to the window near his bed, and peer out across the hospital grounds, following my every footstep with his eyes. It was hard to walk away. Very hard. Glancing back, at dad, I would force my face to smile as I waved again

Occasionally, dad did come home with me for a day or two. Ann was a natural caring nurse and took care of his needs. On one of his visits, I had a labour party meeting I did not want to miss. I had been involved with the labour party for a decade. Dad had raised me red. He had had the same upbringing. Socialism was in our veins. I regularly attended meetings and played my part in supporting the party.

"Do you want to come to the meeting dad?" I asked him. He nodded. So I took dad with me. Man and boy. We sat together in the back of a cold hall, listening to the speaker. It was a long talk. Too long. Dad remained still; his hunched small frame perched on a hard wooden seat. The speaker droned on. And on, and on. We had all had more than enough. Nobody had the courage to stop the record. Nobody but dad. After a thirty minute talk, dad surprised me, the speaker and the entire labour party audience. Sticking his neck out, he boldly spoke his mind. He had always been good at that. Alzheimer's or not, he was going to exercise his tongue. "Wrap it up mate, come on, we've all had enough of you," he told the startled speaker. I laughed into my boots. His honest words had promptly drawn the meeting to a close. Dad got away with it. I didn't lose my labour party membership. Nor did he.

Dad returned to his hospital home a few days later. I continued to visit him twice weekly. It was on one of his visits that he once again got a grip of his old self, and asked me the profound words that opened up this book. I can still hear dad's question.

"In your last moments of life, will you be able to say that the world has been a better place because of your presence?" he enquired, knocking me sideways with the power of his sentence. I filed the question, knowing I must answer it one day. I wasn't ready yet to reply. I had work to do. He had set me a challenge. He had made me think deeply. During other visits, dad remained silent, his life locked inside him, his thoughts shut away. On May 12, 1991, I visited dad for the last time. He was bedridden and had been for a week.

Nurses had gently told me that my father's death was

A hug for dad and the final photo of my father

imminent. Dad was weak, he hadn't been eating, he had an infection, and he lay in bed, his hollowed eyes looking up at me. Searching. Dad had pneumonia.

I held his hand. I had not been there for mum during her last days, but it was a comfort to be there for him. If I had known he would die that night I would not have left his side. Dad slipped away in the early hours of the morning.

It seemed right to give dad a memorable last journey. It was a satisfying moment watching his coffin trail slowly past his beloved Wimbledon FC, the greyhound track and The Grove pub. Those three places had been a large part of his life. If Wimbledon had been playing a home game, I would almost have been tempted to stop the cortege and drive dad into the ground.

Dad had outlived all his brothers. Young Bill was there to pay his respects, reminisce and raise a toast to dad. We all did the same. I still raise a glass or two to my father. I miss him. How I wish he could have been around to witness his beloved grandchildren getting married. Kathryn and Benny in July 1996 and Graeme and Paula in December 1997. They were great occasions he would have enjoyed. I often think of him. He was a good father and a good man. A very good man.

21

The Gift

His name was Jim Ward. He was a solitary soul who had spent twelve years of his life in prison. His crime was the murder of a teenager. When Jim had 'done his bird' I befriended him. Once weekly, we would meet, talk, share a meal and spend time together. Jim was keen to redeem himself. When he died he left me £5,000. "Use it to help disadvantaged youngsters," he had instructed. I promised to honour his wishes. Using Jim's donation, Hope for Children was born, a charity that has helped thousands of youngsters around the world.

I believe in miracles. It's not often £5,000 drops into your lap. In 1994, thanks to Jim Ward, a gentle, non-articulate lonely man I had befriended through the probation service, that wonderful windfall came my way. Jim was on the last lap of his life when he told me that he was leaving his money to me. "I want you to use it to help young people in need," he said.

"I'll do that for you," I told him.

The timing of his donation was perfect. Although I was settled back into my Hemel Hempstead way of life, my experiences in Rwanda were still running through my veins. I could not forget dear Maisie, the inspirational grandma who had devoted her life to looking after orphans. But Maisie, had been refused funding from large charities. She was one of many deserving people who needed backing. Her story, and many others like hers, highlighted the huge, ugly gap in the charity field. I could not turn my back on that need. It was bothering me. Niggling me. Getting under my skin. I had to do something positive for people like Maisie and after much tossing and turning of my thoughts I found the answer. I knew exactly what I wanted to do with Jim's £5,000 donation.

"I want to start a charity Ann," I stated one evening mid way through our dinner. "A charity that supports disadvantaged children."

Ann smiled and chewed over her food and my idea. She knew me well. She knew there was no stopping Bob Parsons. By the time we had finished our meal, I had shared my thoughts. Ann, as always, gave me her support. Over dessert we hatched a plan.

I was going to found a charity that would help smaller projects around the globe. I would begin working in Sri Lanka. I knew the country; I had very good contacts and immediately thought of my loyal friend Tyrrell Cooray who had been a great strength to me during my time in Colombo. We would concentrate on Sri Lanka, and perhaps just one other country.

"We will operate our charity from home," I told Ann. "Our costs will be kept to a minimum. The workforce will be voluntary."

It all seemed so possible. And with hard work, perseverance, my experience, and a good team of people the charity would grow.

"So you won't be retiring then?" Ann joked.

Although I was just four years away from retirement, I was certainly not ready to put my feet up and take it easy. I had so much more to offer than devoting my golden years to planting bulbs in my garden, or idling away the hours pottering round the house or taking holidays in the sun. Instead, I was determined to start a charity. Jim's money would be well spent. So would my retirement years. Little did I realise as I sat in my living room devising a way forward, that in thirteen years time, the charity I was proposing to launch, would have an income of more than one million pounds and would have supported more than 3,000 projects around the globe, giving hope and help to thousands upon thousands of children. No, I certainly would not be retiring. It was not part of my DNA!

22

A Charity is Born

October 23rd 1994. HOPE was officially registered as a charity. There was work to be done. Tins to shake. Funds to raise. Volunteers to motivate and events to organise. Most of all, there were children around the world that needed our help. I was confident we would not let them down.

We started small. But our goal was huge. Our wish list was long. We would not compromise on our aims. We were on a mission to improve the quality of life and advance the rights of children in all corners of the globe. We aimed to bring about positive change on behalf of children and their families. We would also encourage those families to participate in processes that enhance their equality, self-reliance and long-term sustainable development. Wherever possible we would provide practical support allowing children to grow up within their own families and communities. It was a tall order. I always aim high. To make that mission happen, we needed help. And most importantly we needed funding. Strength and a way forward can only be achieved by working together. I set about the challenge of pestering friends and family for support. My repeated requests were like a stuck record. Again and again I sung the same song.

"We've started a charity. Can you help, have you got a few hours to spare?" I would ask repeatedly to everyone I knew. I must have been irritating. Not one person I knew escaped my plea. But it worked. Our very good neighbour, Martin Evans became the treasurer, another true pal, Stephen Phillips took the position of chair, friends became trustees, Ann became the secretary. Many more family members and colleagues crossed the road to avoid me. I was reminded of the cheeky joke about the streets of Aberdeen always being deserted on flag days!

I realised I would have to get used to disappointment. I developed a skin as thick as a rhino. Throwing myself and my money into the charity I worked seven days a week. I was single minded and not prepared to compromise good standards of practice. I led by example and did my best to attract support from near and far.

A street collection with the Mayor, Maureen Flint

Those that didn't rush past me in the street came knocking on our front door, eager to get involved. We called meetings in our living room. We rounded up the troops. And over cups of tea and packets of biscuits we discussed our aims, objectives and mission statement. There was an endless list of 'things to be done'. With energy and enthusiasm we ploughed through them all.

Choosing a name for the charity took time. Endless suggestions were made. Eventually, I proposed we call our new charity HOPE. **H** stood for handicapped, **O** was for orphans,

Chapter 22

P was for poor and **E** for exploited. Those were the four categories of vulnerable children we would be assisting. Heads nodded. Encouraging compliments on the name were made. HOPE was the name and giving hope was the mission. All we needed now was a catchy logo, William Bentley came to our rescue.

One by one we found more and more volunteers keen, eager and willing to give their support to *Hope for Children*. The charity was ready, we were ready, but there was one small hitch. We needed space to carry out our work. Rolling up our sleeves Ann and I began our DIY conversion turning our front room into an international office. All it needed was a computer, a desk, a fax, a cumbersome photocopier and some posters on the wall. We renamed our three-bed semi *HOPE House*. And taking no chances on space we later seized upon an offer by the Mayor of Dacorum, Bert Chapman, to acquire a rent-free garage. Bert also adopted HOPE as his charity of the year. It was a good start. An exciting beginning. I hoped our supporters would grow into a crowd big enough to fill the shed end of Chelsea's football ground. Working from home suited me perfectly. Not only did it minimise costs but was also time effective. Falling out of bed and into the office had never been easier. I could go from pyjamas to pushing a pen at my desk in one minute thirty seconds.

At night, the fax machine would thump and whirr as it received documents from around the world. I felt a warm glow of satisfaction every time I began and ended my day. Our plans were taking shape. Following correspondence with my friend Tyrrell in Sri Lanka we had identified a project in Borella that we would support. It was a centre for street children that I had helped set up when I worked for *Save the Children*. The centre gave these vulnerable children a base to meet, sleep, rest and be fed. It was in threat of closure.

"Under no circumstances should this centre close," I told the HOPE trustees at one of our many meetings.

We unanimously agreed that we would channel our funds into keeping the centre open. I would fly to Sri Lanka and put our plans in motion. Our first project had been identified. In the past I had always visited Sri Lanka on behalf of *Save the Children.* This time, I was flying to Colombo on behalf of my very own charity and at my own expense. It was a deeply satisfying feeling.

Stepping from the plane and into the heat and haze of Colombo, Sri Lanka was like rewinding time. I knew the streets, the faces and the places. I had arranged to meet up with my loyal pal Tyrrell. He had been there for me on so many occasions during my many years working in Sri Lanka for *Save the Children.* He was there for me again, welcoming me to his country and eager to take on his new role as the HOPE representative for Sri Lanka. Tyrrell was perfect for the job. He was the trustworthy man on the ground, the man who could keep an eye on the projects that HOPE would support. We shook hands to seal the new working arrangement and used our time wisely working out a way forward to support the street children project in Colombo. It was the very first project in HOPE's history to receive a grant. Hundreds more would follow. But this was the beginning. The first seeds of HOPE were being planted. With Tyrrell's assistance in Sri Lanka, those seeds would grow to help youngsters in need.

Over the years HOPE has continued to support this important project together with a local partner Sarvodaya. Countless young waifs and strays have been put through education and skills training programmes in Colombo. Learning woodwork and metalwork skills has been a crucial part of their education and future. I know it's made a huge difference to those kids.

I have continued to visit Sri Lanka regularly and have followed their progress with my own two eyes. I've watched those children grow and benefit from the knowledge the project teaches. Skills have been learnt, perfected and put to practical use. Lives have been saved. One of the needy children that came to the centre when he was just eight years old, a young man called Nissan, has gone on to university. He is now a rounded, well-educated, proud and clever individual. The street centre project helped him grow, enabled him to reach his potential. I think of that lad occasionally at the end of the day, I think of the other children and their mothers removed from those dangerous streets of Colombo and benefiting from

Chapter 22

the project. I can sleep well, knowing I tried my best for them.

In the same country we helped support a project FINS, that was producing limbs for amputees. And the more money we spent, the more money we needed to find.

Raising funds quickly became a big part of my life and Ann's. HOPE took over our lives. Most of our weekends were spent shaking tins, public speaking, organising and attending quiz nights or attending local fetes with a HOPE stall. It was a relentless but necessary job. I lost count of the amount of times I would step out with my collection tin, hoping the public would be generous.

Frequently they walked by without putting their hand in their pocket. But occasionally, very occasionally the rewards would be surprisingly large. During one collection at a London railway station, endless commuters rushed past me without a thought for anyone other than themselves and their train home. Then the tide turned. To my surprise, my tin shaking routine reaped a bumper harvest, plus a couple of francs and five pesetas.

The generous donor was a well-dressed city gent. He paused beside me, took time to listen to my request for funds and then, without a second thought he put his hand in his jacket. Either he was going to shoot me, reach for his mobile or make a donation. Thankfully, there was no pistol in his pocket. Instead there was a wallet. A black leather wallet stuffed full of crisp notes and coins.

"Here, take this," he instructed as he pushed the paper money in my hands. "I've just had a bonus at work." Smiling he walked away, happy with his donation.

"Thank you. Thank you very much," I beamed, almost doing handstands of appreciation. Unbelievably, I had just been given £320.00. I counted it three times just to make sure my eyes had not deceived me. They hadn't. The donation was huge. So was the heart of the donor . . . and my smile. I returned to Hemel Hempstead more than happy. That man had reinstated my faith in human nature. During another tin shaking day I received an unexpected subtle compliment. It came from a woman who had paused beside my collection tin to donate her change.

"Thank you very much," I said almost robotically. Half

smiling, she looked up at me and paused a brief moment before offering a reply.

"No, thank you," she said almost correcting me. "It's you and HOPE that are doing the work." I had never thought of my job that way. Her words warmed me. Equally warming was the input from a pool of dedicated volunteers who worked evenings and weekends giving up their time and money to keep the wheels of HOPE turning. Many more local people gave in other ways by sewing bags or knitting teddies, blankets and cardigans for the children in our projects.

One keen volunteer was an elderly lady named Anne Gibbon. Anne was around 85 years old, she was frail, she lived alone, she was not in the best of health, but putting her own ailments to one side, every day without fail, Anne would knit a small teddy bear for the children in our projects. She had the fastest pair of knitting needles in the area and various recipients worldwide hugely appreciated her daily donations. You would not believe how much happiness can be generated from the gift of one bashful looking knitted Ted. For so many children, those teddies are the only toy they have ever owned. Anne knew that, and kept her needles clicking until the very end of her life.

"That's what kept her alive." her son told me at Anne's funeral. Fittingly, he had placed one of her very best knitted teddy's on her coffin.

Some of Anne's teddies in South Africa

Chapter 22

In the early days of HOPE I continued to work for the probation service, commuting daily into London with a briefcase full of letters, faxes and decisions to make for HOPE. I hated spending hours on trains, or waiting for trains, but I used my travelling time wisely, focussing it always on HOPE. In the evening, I devoted hours and energy to HOPE. I had no time to spare but the charity was slowly moving forward, laying down its roots, and achieving its goal to give hope to Handicapped, Orphaned, Poor and Exploited Children.

Ann understood my passion for the children of the planet, and my need to help them grow. Others didn't. They perhaps thought I was just going through a phase that would soon pass.

"When are you going to put your feet up and retire, " they would remark. "Slow down Bob. Have a holiday."

Slowing down, taking it easy or lying horizontal on the Costa del Sol with an ageing population of Brit holidaymakers, was not on my agenda. As soon as I took early retirement from the probation service in 1996, I was working sixteen-hour days for HOPE. There was never enough time in the day to get through my heavy but satisfying workload. I was frequently weary but my heart and head were in exactly the right place. My only wish was that I had been younger when I founded the charity.

HOPE was slowly moving from strength to strength. To make much needed space we built an annexe onto our home. It became a much-needed new office. One of our keen, efficient volunteers, Margaret West was appointed as a local events organiser and was proving to be a keen committed member of the team who would remain with the charity in the years ahead.

We also appointed a specialised fundraiser – Simon Jackman who brought new energy and endless funds to the charity. Simon had begun as a keen volunteer. He put in more than his pound of flesh and worked around the clock, with a mission to make money for the charity. Simon was worth his weight in gold. He was a rare find, a selfless motivated individual who wanted to give more than he wanted to receive and was fundamental in moving HOPE forward. He made our income grow and enabled us to spread our charity wings beyond Sri Lanka.

Simon with mothers processing rice in Ghana

First stop was Zambia. Street children in the city of Livingstone were being rounded up and placed in detention centres. This initiative was led by the local government. They had adopted an 'out of sight, out of mind' attitude and wanted this growing population of begging children tucked away from the eyes of tourists. HOPE wanted to help these vulnerable youngsters.

I flew to Zambia and arranged a meeting with them on the dry dusty streets of the city. I was keen to hear their stories, witness their daily grind and find a way to make their life a notch less miserable.

They gathered swiftly, scurrying towards me from all corners of the city. They were young, wild and worn down by life. Their only means of survival was to beg on street corners or sell their young bodies for sex. The HIV and AIDS epidemic had cruelly wiped out their parents. They were all orphans. AIDS had wiped out a whole generation.

In place of their mothers, grandmothers had stepped in to take care of them. But although the grandmas could serve up plentiful helpings of love, they could not put food on the table. Only 20% of the population had a job. Work went solely to the young and fit. What hope did these grandmothers have of employment? What chance did these weary old ladies have of feeding their grandchildren they loved? What hope did these kids have for a future? I'm an optimist, but the years ahead looked grim.

I visited the grandmothers later that day. There were around two hundred of them, all eager to talk. Immediately I could see that although they were tired from their heavy load in life, they had not given up the fight. Their grandchildren meant the world to them. They wanted to carve out a future for them, but how?

"We want to work," they repeatedly told me. "We want to support our grandchildren and pay for their education," they emphasised. "If they go to school there is hope for their future. But there is no work here for us. We cannot even afford to eat unless our grandchildren beg."

I listened hard to this group of wise women. They had seen life. They had witnessed the premature cruel death of their own children yet they still had energy and hope. They were devoted to their grandchildren and desperate to find a way forward.

HOPE stepped in. HOPE decided to help these women. An income-generating scheme was the answer. If these ladies could make a living, they would be able to hold their heads up high and be self-sufficient.

The scheme was simple, powerful and very cheap to fund. All that was needed from HOPE was a loan of around £100. Just £100 was going to change their lives. That small loan was made available to many of the grandmothers. It would be placed in a kitty for them to take out interest free loans. The lent money would buy them a way to make a small living.

Some of the grandmas would buy sewing machines; others would buy breeding goats or chickens or sell goods on market stalls. When the wheels of their small businesses started to turn, and money was earned, they would be encouraged to pay back their monthly loans for others to use. It was a simple, but effective system. It worked. Within a few months of the scheme beginning, those 200 plucky grandmas were earning a living. They could feed their grandchildren.

Profits were spent on school fees. Instead of begging on street corners, the children had an opportunity of an education. They had a chance of a future. All it took was £100.

Every penny donated to HOPE was quickly spent on direct funding of our projects. We did not believe in having money sitting in our bank. But this fast turnover of income meant that there was always a huge pressure to replace spent funds. I continued to ask friends and family, neighbours, and acquaintances for help. It affected my relationship with many people. I started to look at everyone I knew as a potential supporter for HOPE. I was a little shy about begging for their assistance and helping hands. But I had to. I had made a commitment to the children of the world. I took it seriously and there was no turning back. No amount of rejection would stand in my way. But I quickly learnt that the people with the most money are often quite mean. Those with smaller incomes tended to be the most generous.

My heart would warm every time I opened up an envelope to find a £1 coin wrapped in newspaper or slipped inside a small handwritten letter that had been donated by an OAP. For all I knew, that £1 offering may have been the last £1 of their meagre pension that week. That touching thought and those small genuine donations have continued to lift my spirits over the years with HOPE and keep me motivated. Every £1 matters. Every £1 has been well spent. Every £1 does help make a small difference to individuals and small communities. We had deservedly established a proud reputation as a "no frills" charity. It's a rare characteristic that I'm proud to be part of. I frequently preach the charity motto – your small change can make a big change. It's a simple but true statement. Collectively, small money has bent, shaped and improved so many lives. The major part of all donations go directly to our projects. I pride myself on this truth and keep encouraging everyone both rich and poor to throw his or her money into the HOPE coffers.

I could write endless examples of how small donations have

benefited young lives. Instead I will just tell you about Karoline, a seven-year old orphaned Bangladeshi girl who could not afford her school fees. We donated just £20 to Karoline. £20 was adequate funding to get her educated for a year. She sent us a letter of thanks and her school grades. She has continued to progress with her education. We have continued to support her. £20 made her smile. £20 made Karoline feel she mattered in life.

Karoline's report.

"Take care of the pennies and they turn into pounds" has been a motto installed in me by my mother since my childhood. Thrifty Scottish relatives taught me the meaning of money. I believe in that theory. No donation is too small. Collectively, the pennies turn into pounds. But I'm still hoping for the jackpot and never give up thinking that a generous millionaire may like to offload some of their wealth to HOPE. What a difference that sort of donation would make.

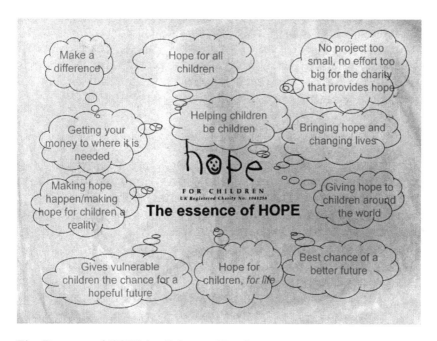

The Essence of HOPE by Rebecca Munds

23

In Sickness and in Health

A heart attack, prostrate cancer, larynx cancer and a melanoma on the arm. I've been through them all and chalked up more than sixty hospital visits in a five-year period. I'm hardly the fittest man on two legs, but as long as I am still breathing, I will continue to work for HOPE.

I'm not afraid of dying. I can say that with my hand on my heart. I don't fear death. I just fear that my health folds before I have achieved everything I want to do in life. That is my main concern. That is what keeps me fighting back when illness strikes and slows me down. I don't give in. I don't give up. I try my hardest to get back on track. Health is everything. I've had a good track record of health through my life. But as I approached my more mature years, I began to chalk up my fair share of hospital visits.

My first health scare came in 1998 at a rugby match in Twickenham. I'd gone to the match with two friends, Keith and Stuart Hutcheson who were visiting from South Africa. I did the driving, and we talked sport all the way. I was looking forward to an afternoon of rugby and the chance to sing a few anthems and soak up the atmosphere.

But climbing several flights of stairs in the stadium to reach our seats, I felt unusually breathless. My chest was tight. The ascent was an effort, but I kept my concerns to myself and blamed the heat. A top class game of rugby kept my mind from worrying too hard. But I knew internally I was not at my peak.

I don't remember the score at that match, but I do remember that as I drove home, I sensed something inside me was worryingly wrong. My breathing was different and my chest ached. Dropping my friends at home, I pointed the car straight towards the Accident and Emergency Department of my local hospital. Twenty minutes later, parking the vehicle, I booked myself in. It was a decision that may have just saved my life. I was in the right place at the right time when, moments after my arrival at hospital, I suffered a minor heart attack. It took seconds to take hold of my body. I blacked out. When I came round I was on the floor of the A & E ward with nurses and doctors by my side calmly taking care of me.

In St Peter's ward, tests revealed the heart attack. I had an irregular heartbeat that had caused the problem. I lay on my hospital bed, staring up at the ceiling with more than enough time to think. I felt glad to be alive and was immediately reminded of one of my probationers who was a drug addict. He had often told me that his greatest pleasure was to wake up each morning realising that he had been granted another day in life. Now I fully understood him. I was relieved my attack had been minor and I could look to another day, but I did not want to spend too long in bed. I had meetings in the morning, phone calls to make, reports to prepare.

"You must slow down, take it easy," I was told by doctors. Ann repeated their words, concerned by my health scare. I agreed to listen to medical advice. Just for a day or two.

On day three, I returned to my desk, the fax machine, my diary of appointments, the phone that always rings and the fundraising events that stretched ahead. I didn't think too hard about the possibility of having a second heart attack, I didn't think too hard about my own health. I just kept going and hoped my well-worn ticker would do the same. But I was deeply relieved when, twelve months later, doctors agreed to fit me with a pacemaker.

It's an ingenious device, smaller than a matchbox. Inside is a battery connected to leads that pass through the veins to the ventricle of my heart. If my heartbeat becomes irregular, the pacemaker kicks in and does its job.

Chapter 23

I barely know its there. But that incredible minute machine is one of the greatest inventions of medical science. It enables me to live my life and I do that just a little bit harder as every year passes. With the pacemaker in place, I sold my car and walked as much as possible. I stopped worrying about my heart and concentrated on the worries of the charity. We always have money to find. Fundraising is the foundation of everything we do.

With that thought in mind, I pushed myself back into working at full throttle. Working is what I do best. Using my time and energy to help others keeps me strong and keeps me going. Too many old people are killed off simply because they don't have a purpose. Whatever our age, I believe we can contribute to our fellow beings.

So I sailed towards my seventies, pacemaker in place. But just around the corner was another medical hill I had to climb . . . and that was cancer. Yes, the dreaded C word reared its ugly head just four years after my pacemaker was fitted. A routine MOT health check and a PSA blood test with my GP revealed I had prostate cancer. I remember the day the bad news was broken. It was not the best day of my life. Cancer is such a huge word. It scared me. Had the cancer spread or was it containable? As always, when my chips are down, I internalise my fears and emotions and just face my problem head on.

"What are my options? " I boldly asked the doctor.

"Chemotherapy or surgery," was his reply.

"Cut it out," I said, without hesitation. "As soon as possible."

A week later, I was admitted to Watford General Hospital for surgery. Three days later I was home again . . . recovering at my desk! Those three days were more than enough to lie around dwelling on my future. I am not a good patient; I am best out of bed. That's how I handle illness. I get back on my feet as quickly as possible and return to my busy schedule.

I put that same theory into practice when cancer struck again in 2005. A persistent croaky throat had prompted me to visit my doctor. I was referred to hospital for a biopsy. A tumour was found on my larynx. How long it had been nestling there I do not know. I was in total shock. We always think these things happen to other people. It was my turn. For once I felt briefly sorry for myself. Anger was let loose in my veins. I simply didn't have time to tackle cancer again, but I had no choice.

"Get it out," was my response to the unwelcome news. I did not want the dreaded cancer to spread. Surgery was not an option. Instead I faced 33 continuous sessions of radiotherapy at the University College Hospital in London.

Every day I took the train from Hemel to the radiotherapy department of the hospital. For twenty minutes, I underwent the painless but gruelling treatment. Lying still in the radiotherapy room, a mask would be fitted over my face. The mask ensured the treatment would be concentrated on exactly the same spot every day of my radiotherapy. Keeping my head straight the radiation began. Beam me up Scottie!

During my recovery time I did not lie back and feel sorry for myself. Instead, I occupied my mind with HOPE paperwork. It kept me focussed, kept me going through this long arduous ordeal. But radiotherapy is exhausting. The treatments and travel left me tired and lethargic. In my low moments I could not help but ask the question "why me?" It was a testing time. I lost my voice, I lost my taste buds but I did not lose my will and determination to get better.

Life without a voice for six months was almost unbearable. Whispering was the only frustrating solution. I can laugh now at the amount of times I answered the phone with my pathetically weak voice.

"Hello," I whispered down the line. "Hello," I repeated, trying my hardest to turn up my own volume. It was impossible. My voice was so soft that even those with acute radar hearing would struggle to hear me. Callers, unable to detect I was there, would simply slam the phone down leaving me in a state of frustration. Then the phone would ring again and the whole process would be repeated. I didn't even have the voice to moan about the incident. Frustration was always a whisper away.

I was not the easiest person to live with during that episode of my life. Ann, as always took my medical hiccup in her stride and kept smiling. If the pressure of my illness weighed heavy

Chapter 23

on her mind, she took refuge in the local Women's Institute. Perhaps, she also survived this gruelling episode by taking great delight in the fact that for once, I was not able to answer her back! But silence for me was not golden.

Speaking engagements on behalf of HOPE were even harder to get through. I did my best. I became the best public whisperer for miles. Even with a microphone, my voice was diluted to such a soft level that my audience had no choice but to hang onto my every word. The hard of hearing had no chance when I did my low volume speeches.

Losing my voice was hard to cope with, but midway through my treatment I also lost my taste buds. Miserable was my middle name. Without the joy of taste I lost weight. Food had lost its appeal. I turned my back on the best steaks, the best cakes and even my favourite food of all time . . . kippers. Food seems pointless when you can't taste. My weight dropped. So did my morale. Staying positive took effort. I remained strong by focussing always on getting to the last day of my treatment. I had that date marked on the calendar – January 25th 2006. I was counting down. It was a date that was as important as the day I left national service. I welcomed it with all my heart and soul.

Walking out of the hospital on the last day of radiotherapy was an accomplishment. I had climbed my own mountain. My final bout of radiotherapy was over. I celebrated. Quietly. At home. With Ann and my thoughts. I thank my lucky stars that radiotherapy served its purpose and kicked the cancer out of my body. Monthly check ups at the hospital with a wonderful consultant, Tova Prior, are part of my life now. Every time I get an all clear, I look forward to the next chunk of life and do my utmost to make sure I use that time wisely.

As for my voice . . . well, thankfully it slowly returned. Apart from the occasional cough, it became strong as it ever was before the cancer. I keep it in good working order. The occasional beer and glass of wine helps oil the vocal chords. I continue to deliver speeches for HOPE. I continue to talk incessantly over the phone on behalf of HOPE, and of course, when I get the chance to watch Chelsea at Stamford Bridge

I make sure I join in with all the chants. My taste buds have almost fully returned. They are not quite what they used to be, but to salivate over kippers again and then enjoy every morsel was a big bonus in life.

Yet, just when you think you've climbed the cancer mountain, another peak arises and its time to start the ascent once again. In March 2007 I found myself facing cancer scare number three. Alarm bells were raised when I noticed moles on my arms and leg that looked worrying. I tried to ignore my limbs. Who was I kidding? Every time I unpeeled my clothes, the moles were there, two of them. Big. Bold. Ugly and growing. I knew they were abnormal. So did my doctor. He referred me to a dermatologist. Sample cells were taken from my arm and leg. One week later, I got the test results.

My leg was fine. But my arm was far from fine. I had a malignant growth. Melanoma. To say the word melanoma is simply a more polite gentle way of dropping the bombshell. I had cancer of the skin. All my years of being in hot climates had gone against me.

I confess I have always been a bit of a sun worshipper. Soaking up vitamin D and feeling the heat has been part of my life. In Sri Lanka I was exposed to the sun morning, noon and night. It was the same in so many of the countries I visited on behalf of *Save the Children*. Sun-tan lotion was not in vogue until recent years. I must admit, I did not slap on a factor forty every time I set foot outside the door. Too late. I had melanoma. I needed to have it cut out quickly and hope it had not spread to other parts of my body.

Time is crucial when it comes to cancer. Tackle it fast and you stand a chance. Sit back and ignore it and the cancer grows. I didn't want to waste a second. The only way to guarantee immediate surgery was to go against all my socialist principals and 'go private'. Paying for medical treatment guarantees speed. It felt wrong to join the elite band of people who can put their hands in their back pocket and pay for their health. Equality in a health service should be the right for everyone.

I remember spending time in New York in 1966. I was on a placement with the probation service and working with youths in the seedier side of Queens. One black lad in my care broke his ribs. I took him to the nearby hospital. As soon as we walked into the hospital the segregation began. Two doors divided the rich and the poor. One door led to the 'free treatment'. The other door led to the 'private treatment'.

We joined the queue for the free treatment. It was 100 bodies long, snaking its way through corridors. The weak and the wounded propped themselves up and patiently waited. And waited. We took six hours to see the doctor. And while the hours passed I studied the other door. There was no queue to see the private doctor who sat behind the 'private' door. Every patient who could afford to pay for treatment was seen immediately and within a few minutes of arrival they were on the road to recovery. It was shocking to witness the imbalance. I returned to the UK a proud committed supporter of our National Health Service and the equality it provided to all.

But at the age of 74, it was now time for me to walk through the private treatment door for my melanoma. I struggled to take this route to the operating theatre but to wait for my free NHS place was far too worrying. I wanted the cancer out of my body and I wanted it out NOW. Not in a months time or more.

"You're worth it," Ann said encouragingly. An appointment was made promptly. One week later I was under anaesthetic. Skin from my leg would be grafted onto my arm to help heal the huge hole left by surgery. But I did not have time for healing. I had diary appointments to attend.

"Is it okay to fly to Hong Kong next week?" I asked my doctor. On my mind was a HOPE function. I was determined to be there to deliver a speech and raise the profile of HOPE. I was also taking a flight to visit my son and his family in Australia. But my doctor was anxious.

"Not a good idea," he stated. "The surgery wound may take time to heal." It was not what I wanted to hear. Usually I charge forward in times of illness but this time round I was going to take my recovery seriously and not take chances. Putting myself first was a rare occurrence. But it was a wise move. I healed without problems. And the post operation tests thankfully revealed the cancer had not spread. Apart from a hole in my arm big enough to fit a plum, I could put cancer behind me again. The relief was immeasurable.

"You're a survivor," I was told a couple of weeks later by a friend of the charity. I never thought of myself that way. But perhaps she was right. I had scraped through a brush with cancer yet again. I had survived.

HA x 1 + C x 3 = 60 HV is an amusing equation that sprung to mind recently and is a neat reminder of my health scares and my survival.

HA = heart attack.
C = cancer.
HV = hospital visits.

Whichever way you look at it, I am still going strong and hoping the equation does not grow. I'm thankful I can wake up each morning, enjoy a brand new day and make the most of my time. But these cancer scares have left me a little shaken and more cautious with my health. For the first time in my life, I have invested in a bottle of factor fifty lotion, and a floppy hat. I have to remind myself to use them. When the heat is on, I now ration my basking time to just thirty minutes. And as well as staying in the shade, I avoid inhaling other peoples smoke, which I believe was the cause of my cancer of the larynx and I welcome the recently enforced 'no public smoking ban.'

I don't want to take any chances with my health and pay far more attention to every ache and pain in my body. Somewhere, at the back of my mind, and occasionally at the front, I always have the fear that cancer will return. I thought good things came in threes. Is that the same for bad things? Have I had my quota now? I remain vigilant and consider myself very lucky to be around. Very lucky.

24

The Wave that Shocked the World

Boxing Day 2004. The news was bad. A tsunami had devastated the coastline of Sri Lanka and India. Many other countries were also suffering. The death toll was alarmingly high. HOPE responded immediately and reached out to help. Our relief programme was to be the biggest event in the history of HOPE.

Standing outside our local Sainsbury's supermarket on a crisp December morning I gently shook my HOPE collection bucket and prayed the public were feeling generous. HOPE was raising funds for the victims of the tsunami. Beside me, a team of HOPE volunteers were doing the same. Collecting on the streets is often a game of luck. Sometimes you can stand for hours and come home virtually empty handed. Today was a different story. Today, Joe Public was keen to help rebuild the millions of lives that had been shattered by the devastating wave. Coins rattled. Notes jumped. Our buckets began to fill. Shoppers offloaded their change and their emotions. It seemed that almost everyone had been affected by the news of the tsunami.

Many countries had been affected by this destructive wave. Its impact had shocked the world. In my hometown of Hemel Hempstead, the generosity was touching. In addition to our supermarket sweep, on the front page of the local newspaper we appealed for funds. We also took our collection buckets to shops, colleges and schools. Money steadily poured in.

The tsunami had claimed victims in Sri Lanka and India where we had worked for many years. The media coverage was immeasurable. Stories of survival against the odds unfolded. Stories of death and devastation were viewed on our television screens. Appeals were made. Money poured into numerous charities. Nationally, a Disaster Emergency Committee (DEC) appeal was established. But HOPE fundraised independently. We were not members of DEC and their rules and regulations excluded us from receiving any funding. Therefore, we were going solo and there was no time to lose.

Every second counts when disaster strikes. That important principle had been part of my Disaster and Management Training in Bangkok many years ago. It had stayed with me. So while the DEC funds grew (raising in excess of £350 million), our collection buckets grew heavier. Additionally, a huge much appreciated donation of £76,000 from the ESC (Entertainment Software Company) landed in our lap to be spent solely on tsunami relief work. It was the biggest single donation our charity had ever received. We needed that money more than ever. Miracles do come when you need them.

HOPE made an immediate grant available to the disaster. We concentrated our relief efforts on Sri Lanka and India. We did not have direct contacts with other affected countries.

The death toll was shocking. In Sri Lanka, 30,000 had died. 15,212 were injured. 422,255 were displaced and living in 443 different camps. These were distressing statistics. Equally distressing were the 700 children who were orphaned and the 3,409 who had lost one parent. Tyrrell Cooray and his local team were immediate in their response. Four days after the disaster we were able to provide milk powder and household utensils to numerous families.

In Tamil Nadu in South India, 9,886 died, 3,324 were injured, 499,962 were displaced and living in 412 camps. Our representative, Rakesh Mittal and his steering committee ensured that we were one of the first charities on the scene.

Cancelling my own festive family appointments I concentrated my energy on tsunami relief work. We began a series of phone calls to Sri Lanka hatching a plan to help the orphans of the tsunami. My long-term contacts in the country were at the heart of the disaster. Their advice was solid and vital. HOPE had the infrastructure to get into Sri Lanka immediately and offer a crucial helping hand.

Just two weeks after disaster struck, I was flying out to Colombo with £100,000 to spend on tsunami relief work. HOPE was setting up a scheme for all the orphans of the tsunami. HOPE was going to fund foster parents for all the children who had lost their parents in the disaster. Siblings would remain together and not be sent to separate institutions. I was very committed towards 'care in the community' and had led a move to close Childrens Homes as a member of the Social Services Committee on the County Council. I had also researched the affects of Institutionalisation of Children for my Ph.D thesis.

With this knowledge in mind I set to work. Under the guidance of social workers all foster parents would be interviewed, selected and approved for the scheme under Fit Person Orders and then financially supported by HOPE for three years. This would later be extended to five years. Trauma counselling would also be made available for the children in need. There were so many children left psychologically damaged, bewildered, devastated, homeless, orphaned and vulnerable.

An orphan with his foster parents and social worker

One of those children was a sweet-faced young girl called Sobani. I met her and many others in Batticaloa, a coastal town that had been devastated by the tsunami. The whole area was flattened. The sea had swallowed up houses, boats, people and animals and spat them out in its path of destruction. Debris lined the shores. It was a shocking unforgettable scene.

Sobani was a lucky survivor. Both her parents had been swept away to their death. Sobani had been spared. She wore a harrowed expression. Fear was stamped on her face. Like so many of the children and adults in her area, she was terrified that another wave may rage through her community. The sea she had once loved was now the enemy. She stayed away from the shore.

Sobani was one of so many tsunami orphans in great need of love, security and family life to help her come to terms with the disaster. She needed all the help she could get to face a future without her mum and dad. Life would never be the same again for Sobani, but with the help of HOPE she had a chance to rebuild her shattered life.

We were going to place her with foster parents who would provide her with the stability and love she needed. Beneath the hot midday sun, Sobani and 17 other tsunami orphans met their new foster parents for the first time. From the sidelines, I watched the emotional encounters. There had been so many families that had come forward volunteering to be foster parents. Some of them had lost children of their own.

Some were grandparents. The tsunami may have destroyed lives and homes but it had not crushed the spirit of the community. In the face of disaster families were reaching out to help each other.

In Sri Lanka, HOPE went on to help every one of the tsunami orphans find foster parents. The families selected for the scheme would receive financial support for five years. We also built and equipped eighteen pre-school buildings that are in the Camps. In India we concentrated on the worst affected areas in Tamil Nadu. We also built new pre-schools and low cost houses in two villages. The villages have both been called HOPE.

Chapter 24

I revisited our tsunami relief projects again nine months after the disaster. The recovery process was slow but I was impressed with the courage, tenacity and optimism of so many people who had lost families, friends, homes, possessions and employment. Chris and Rangi Stubbs are two of those people who deserve praise and recognition for their work. For many years, they have tirelessly worked helping disabled children and their parents both throughout the civil war and the tsunami. They have established two centres in Nuwara Eliya and Batticaloa, which embrace the needs of children who have been 'written off' by authorities. HOPE has supported their work over the years. The list of children and parents they have helped is long.

Our fostering scheme remains in place and is working well for the children. The psychological healing process will take many years to resolve, but we will continue to be there for the children when the media coverage fades. That's important.

I am personally proud of HOPE's huge contribution to the relief effort and the speed at which we stepped in to help. When the tsunami struck, many of our Sri Lankan, Indian and UK volunteers and staff cancelled their festive activities, and instead gave their time and efforts to raising funds and undertaking relief work. I did the same. How could I sit back and relax over post Christmas meals and gatherings when there was so much work to be done for the victims of this natural disaster. HOPE did not hesitate to offer a huge helping hand. We did not waste time. We did not waste funds on hotel bills and flights. For my immediate visit to Sri Lanka I paid my own air fare and stayed in very basic accommodation and with good friends in Colombo making sure every penny raised by HOPE was for the orphans of the tsunami. It's a warming thought that HOPE has given hope to so many orphans. Perhaps in the future, I may return to Batticaloa and meet Sobani again. Perhaps a smile has returned to her face and with the help of her foster parents she has rebuilt her life and found a way to heal her broken heart. I do hope so.

Tsunami relief work

Building a HOPE Village

25

International Grandchildren

Slippers and kippers and nights of interrupted sleep! It's all part of being a grandad and it's a role I embrace as often as possible. Nothing quite beats being a grandfather.

A large chunk of my life has been spent looking after the needs of children around the world. That's what I do best. I have lost count of how many youngsters I have helped along the way. They are all important to me. Every one of them. I have stepped into their lives briefly with *Save the Children* or when I am visiting HOPE projects in all corners of the globe. Their stories of survival and their innocent and sometimes haunted faces touch me deeply. I do my best for them all. But then I must walk away, board a plane and fly home. I cannot get personally attached or emotionally involved. Instead I hand the day-to-day responsibility to someone else. It's the nature of my job.

But there are half a dozen very special children that remain in my life constantly. I can spoil and love them wholeheartedly and follow their progress in life. I can hold them in my arms, call them on the phone, look at their photos scattered round my living room and share precious times together. These six lively kids are my grandchildren. Three of them – my daughter's offspring, Sarah Ming, Matthew and Charlie Becker live in Germany, the other three Jack, Joe and Finn are my son's lads. They live on the other side of the world in Sydney, Australia.

It's hardly surprising I have international grandchildren.

Both my children fled the nest and travelled, worked and settled down abroad. Kathryn married a German, Benny who worked for Bayers Pharmaceutical. Graeme married an Irish girl, Paula. Their paths in life led them overseas. Kathryn went to Africa where she met Benny, then to Taiwan, China, Dominican Republic and Germany. Graeme to Hong Kong to work for the Bank of America - where he met Paula. From the Far East they settled down under in Australia. We miss them. Yet it would be selfish of me to wish they were living on my doorstep. They all have happy, satisfying lives and have settled in great environments to raise their children.

Of course, distance keeps us apart. But despite the miles, I try my best to keep up with my children and grandchildren as much as possible. I've made several trips to Australia to visit my family down under. And several more journeys to Germany to see the other three grandchildren. And whenever we get time together, I pull on my grandad slippers, and do my best to influence them positively. A bag of pick and mix sweets from the corner shop generally helps. There's nothing like liquorice laces, sherbet fountains or gobstoppers to gain popularity and attention!

They call me grandad. Or grandad Bob. I like that. They pick up the phone and ring. They send me drawings, cards, little letters and photos. They keep me young and show me the world through their eyes.

I remember a gentle stroll I took to the shops with my daughter's children during their last visit. We were heading for the sweet counter of the newsagent with 10 pence each to spend on pick and mix. Along the way, one of the children pointed up at two plastic bags that had been blown into a tree. The branches had seized the bags holding them tight as if they were part of the foliage.

"Look grandad, look," they chorused pointing up in amazement. I did as I was told, glanced upwards and smiled.

"That's a plastic bag tree," I stated. "You don't see them very often in England. I never saw one at all when I was young. They really are quite rare." Their innocent heads turned to look back at me. They did not question my information. As far as they were concerned they had just passed a rare plastic bag tree in blossom. That tree became the talk of the day. Everything was possible in their world. It does me good to think that way.

The plastic bag tree!

Last Christmas I pulled on my thermals and accompanied my daughter's children on a trip to Lapland to see Father Christmas. Ann was by my side. Shivering. We travelled a long way on husky-pulled sledges to see the white bearded old man. We braved crisp winter snow and an exhausting schedule. But watching my three grandchildren glow with joy when they met Santa was a cherished moment. Precious. Memorable. Satisfying. If only Santa could have given me a sack full of energy as an early Christmas present.

In the summer of 2007, all the grandchildren came to stay. We had one glorious but chaotic month under one roof. Ann was in her element. I was in the sweet shop or playing football in the garden with them as much as possible. I encourage physical activity with my grandchildren as it helps them and me to sleep longer! We took a week out together at Center Parcs in Wiltshire. Instead of being Bob Parsons, MBE, founder of Hope for Children and international traveller, I was simply grandad. Nothing else mattered except having fun. And what a week we had. We swam, rode bikes, fed the ducks and the squirrels that crept up to the patio doors of our woodland nestled bungalow. Exhausted was an understatement. The words "goodnight grandad," was music to my ears at the end of every day. But I would not have missed this time for all the tea in China.

Off to Center Parcs,
out of picture Benny and Paula

I can only hope my grandchildren grow up to care for their world, people and for each other. I am confident they will. Perhaps I have influenced them in some small way. Little Matthew is already taking after grandad. He likes kippers chess, cricket and football. Jack is a keen swimmer and rugby player. All of the grandchildren have gentle, kind hearts. It's a good start!

Graeme, Finn, Paula, Joe and Jack

Kathryn, Charlie, Matthew, Benny and Sarah Ming

26

A Decade Later

Ten years of giving. Ten years of fund raising. A decade of doing our best for the children of the world. It was time to celebrate HOPE's achievements. We organised a champagne reception at 10 Downing Street. Cherie Booth made us more than welcome.

Cherie Booth presents a collage to me

Proud and self satisfied, I climbed the stairs of 10 Downing Street. I was walking in the footsteps of history. Winston Churchill, Harold Wilson, Margaret Thatcher and Tony Blair, the prime minister at the time, had walked the very same steps. Their portraits hung on the walls. Every leader had enjoyed their significant moments at Number 10. But today

Chapter 26

was HOPE's great moment. We were celebrating our tenth year in 2004. We were looking back at a decade of achievement and looking forward to a future of supporting children in need around the world.

Forty VIP guests had been invited to attend our ten-year celebrations. Volunteers, staff, supporters, trustees, beneficiaries and celebrities gathered in the very grand Downing Street guest lounge. A hum of happiness reverberated round the room. I shook hands with Michael Parkinson, who had come to show his support for HOPE. I chatted to another invited celebrity, Rachel Stevens who was also keen to add her clout to our charity.

Over the past decade, many big name celebrities have given their time and celebrity muscle to HOPE. Gary Lineker, Justin Rose and Lulu are patrons of the charity. Yachtsman, Seb Clover and many more big and small names in the media have also added their support.

"If by working with HOPE I can make a very small contribution, then that is an achievement which far outstrips the satisfaction of breaking a sailing record." Seb Clover commented when he became a patron in 2003.

We don't demand too much from our celebrities but every week of the year, the demands we have made on our supporters, volunteers and trustees have been huge. It is this army of unrecognised people who keep HOPE afloat. We invited as many of them as possible to the Downing Street celebration. Rachel Pierce, our chair of trustees was glowing with pride, a smile permanently painted on her face.

Like so many of our supporters, she has devoted hours and energy to HOPE. Today, she could have a moment to reflect, relax and celebrate. Every one of our invited guests could also raise their wine glass knowing they had made a major mark in the progress of HOPE.

The clink of champagne glasses, and a gentle murmur of conversation filled the room. Never in my wildest dreams could I have imagined that when I founded HOPE ten years ago, that I would be standing at Number 10, a decade later, having raised nearly half a million pounds for **h**andicapped, **o**rphaned, **p**oor and **e**xploited children. Never would I have believed that our charity would have grown so significantly.

We waited in anticipation for our reception host, Cherie Booth. She was running late. Her work as a barrister had caused the delay. It didn't matter. The moment she strode into the room, she shone. Her charm and professionalism were commendable. She smiled. She chatted and then paid tribute to HOPE, with a very fine well-constructed speech.

"Its not often I get the pleasure to offer a reception in honour of such a unique charity as *Hope for Children*," she began. My heart was instantly warmed. If only my dad could have seen me at that moment in time. It was enough to make him rise from his grave.

Cherie continued, giving a précis of HOPE's work, its mission and commitment to underprivileged children. She talked about how HOPE retains slim UK administration costs and she encouraged supporters to fill in the recently launched £10 for ten months donation forms to help HOPE's growth in the near future.

The collage

A ripple of heartfelt applause followed her speech. I stepped forward to be presented with a framed photo collage that had captured my work over the past decade. I too gave a speech. Not too brief. Not too long. I thanked many people for helping me achieve more than I had ever dreamt possible. I recalled significant moments in my life, including the personal privileged meetings I'd had with Mother Teresa and Nelson Mandela. Both were humbling experiences. Their non-judgemental attitudes and humility had made a lasting impression on my career. But it wasn't just Mr Mandela and Mother Teresa that had helped me on my great journey through life and with HOPE. I thanked everyone and felt joyful. Satisfied. Happy anniversary HOPE.

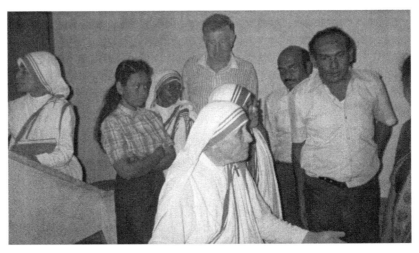

My meeting with Mother Teresa in Colombo, 1989.

Over the past decade, HOPE has received many other awards. Not quite enough to fill a trophy cabinet, but we have certainly made our mark nationally and locally. In 2005 the London Rotary Club recognized HOPE's contribution to the community and also put me forward for a Paul Hunter Fellow award and nominated me for an entry in Who's Who. Simon well deservedly picked up *Charity Fundraiser of the Year* award in 2001. And in 2006, I was nominated to receive the Freeman of the Borough Award in my area.

Very few people receive this title locally. I have to confess I am not sure what it truly means to be a Freeman except that throughout history it gives recipients grazing rights in the area. I don't have a flock of sheep. I don't even have a dog now, but I was proud to step forward and be a Freeman. My daughter secretly flew in from Germany for the occasion. We celebrated at a reception with the mayor. But as always, whenever I shake hands and receive an award, I praise everyone in HOPE and do not selfishly take the glory.

"I couldn't have done this on my own," I announced, at the presentation reception. I just happen to be the lead person and the founder of the charity. HOPE would not have grown over the years without everyone's contribution."

The Freeman of the Borough framed award hangs in my hallway at home. The photo collage of our tenth year anniversary is mounted in the corner of the living room. The numerous pictures within its frame are a reminder of the huge effort we have made over the years to help children. There are photos of me shaking collection tins; other snaps show me with my arms around children at our projects in Sri Lanka, Africa, UK and Europe. As the saying goes – every picture tells a story.

My very own Royal Mail stamp

Chapter 26

When I have the time, I reminisce on every one of those photos. The smiles, the handshakes and the moments in HOPE's history. But not one of those captured, photographed moments can show the depth of joy that runs through my veins when I take time out to visit a HOPE project. It is only then, walking into a shanty slum, a tin roofed township home, or a one-roomed basic school in a far-flung corner of the globe, that I can truly appreciate the difference our money has made. That indescribable, unique feeling is what keeps me committed to my work for HOPE. It's what gets me out of bed every morning to do my daily best for the charity. It's what gets me out in the wind and rain to collect funds for HOPE. As corny as it may sound the joy and satisfaction gained from visiting projects is what makes everything worthwhile. (Gap years for students should be compulsory!) Years of shaking cans and fundraising, years pestering companies, friends and contacts for funds and years motivating volunteers and working night and day. It's all worth it when you see the fruits of your labour. If anyone wonders why I don't sit back and take it easy, I would invite them to accompany me on a trip to a South African township to spend time with some HIV orphans, or come visit a street children project in Sri Lanka or the Philippines and then they will truly understand Bob Parsons and what makes him tick.

A township crèche supported by HOPE

HOPE is not the charity it was in 1994. Every year I have watched it grow. With growth comes the pressure to raise more funds. But we have risen to the challenge to keep the money coming in and established several annual events that fill up the huge HOPE moneybox.

The Edinburgh Marathon is one of those events. For the past four years, we have been one of the official charities for the marathon. In 2007, more than two hundred runners pulled on their jogging shoes and sweated their way through the demanding 26 mile route to raise more than £90,000 for HOPE.

Our Marathon de Sables sponsored team in Africa

Rossgate School Choir sing 'Song of HOPE'
Composed by Thomas Evans

Suzie and Thomas Evans perform for HOPE

Rob Ambrose completes a Unicycle Sponsored Ride in a new Guinness Book of Records time

A Burns Night Supper, Quiz and Race Evenings, concerts, charity lunches, sponsored swims by disabled children from the Dolphins Club in Hemel Hempstead, the London Marathon and an annual 26-mile sponsored walk organised by one of our Patrons – Nadia Howell, have all become institutionalised dates in the HOPE diary. The HOPE ball at Grosvenor House, Mayfair has also become an important source of fundraising. It's a grand evening when I get the chance to wear a kilt, eat like a king, and sit back and watch a fabulous evening of entertainment. David Simpson, with our hardworking committee members including Helen McMillan, Rebecca Munds, Julian Skeens, Rob Common and Jennifer Phillips, organise the ball, pulling in thousands of pounds for HOPE.

Every year the roots of HOPE grow deeper. With expansion, comes change and turbulence. In 2004, we had grown to such a level that we could barely keep up with the work. We were bulging out of the office annexe attached to my home. We had decisions to make to maintain our progress. Should we hold onto our small tin shaking, home grown grassroots amateur image, or expand into a more upmarket charity with salaried staff and proper premises?

The trustees met. Discussions unfolded. Unanimously, we decided we must let HOPE grow and spread its wings. There were so many children out there in the world that needed our help. If we expanded, we could support even more projects worldwide. We would appoint salaried staff. We would move our office to independent premises away from the house. Simon Jackman would be promoted to Chief Executive. Margaret West, Migena Kovacs and Jay Halligan were appointed and the bar would be raised even higher on our fund raising targets. With a great team of staff and volunteers, together with £125,000 I received from friends and contacts, we were able to reach our 2006/7 target of one million pounds.

Tyrrell at his farewell event in February 2007.

HOPE continues to make its mark in the world because of so many dedicated people including our strong force of supporters and our overseas representatives.

My loyal friend Tyrrell Cooray is one such representative who has done so much for the charity. In 1994 he set up HOPE in Sri Lanka. On December 31st 2006 he retired. He is a really great man. Together with Simon Jackman and Rachel Pierce I flew to Sri Lanka for his farewell gathering. We applauded him. Loudly. He had done so much for others.

Change is not always easy. I have to let go. I have to hand over some responsibility and pass on the HOPE baton. It's not easy for me. I struggle to step aside and let others step forward. But I'm slowly, very slowly adjusting to change as President and I have no regrets that we did the right thing. I look forward to HOPE's 15th anniversary in 2009. I can't think of anything else I would rather be doing with my life.

27

Sharon's Washing Machine

Her name was Sharon. She had a heart bigger than her humble township home. In her care were fifteen orphans. Many of them were HIV positive. Sharon cooked for them, cared for them and kept them clean. Her standards were high. Every day, she spent three long hours washing endless items of their clothing by hand. It was just one of the chores she had to face daily. "Could you use a washing machine?" I asked Sharon. She smiled. HOPE bought this remarkable lady the much-needed machine. It's a small gift but it's made a huge difference to Sharon's life.

In May 2007, before this book was completed, I made a third trip to South Africa to visit some of HOPE's projects. I stayed in Cape Town. My schedule, as always, was fast and furious. I wanted to pack as much as possible into my one week. HOPE supports twelve projects in the Cape Town area of South Africa. Most of them are pre-school crèches. In these cramped but much needed crèches, young children are left in the capable arms of the caring managers while their mothers go to work. There is no social benefit system in South Africa. If you don't work, you don't eat. It's that simple. Mothers must leave their children in crèches. Often from early morning to late at night. There is no other option.

Most crèches are basic. Sometimes, up to 70 youngsters are crowded into one room where they will play, learn, sleep and eat. Frequently, they lack toilet facilities, play equipment, and trained staff. But their role is vital.

By chance, wandering round the township of Mitchells Plains, my footsteps led me towards Sharon's crèche and care centre. Although facilities were barely adequate, I was immediately impressed by Sharon and her devotion to the children in her care. Out of the goodness of her heart, she had opened the doors of her township dwelling and taken in fifteen orphans. Can you imagine that happening in your own neighbourhood? It's highly unlikely, but in South Africa it's not an uncommon situation. Communities help each other. Women come together and offer love and support where it is needed.

Sharon was inspirational. But she was clearly struggling. There was not enough time in the day for her to complete her heavy load. In the time I spent with Sharon she did not have a second to spare. She was running fast constantly trying to keep up with the demands of so many youngsters. She did her best.

I talked to Sharon as she laboriously washed the children's clothes. She used a huge tin tub. Rolling up her sleeves she scrubbed and rinsed and wrung out countless items of clothing. While she hung the clothes to dry, her flock of orphans played, demanded, cried, laughed and tugged at her hand. They tugged at my heart. I saw her switch from washerwoman to mother, cook, cleaner and provider. Her only help came from a neighbour. Every day of the year, and without a holiday, Sharon faced the same ritual. She was one of South Africa's many unsung heroines. There are many women like Sharon, scattered across the townships and villages of South Africa, all doing what they can for the children. In South Africa, the AIDS epidemic has wiped out so many mothers. Orphans are everywhere. Many of those orphans, like the children in Sharon's care were HIV positive. It's a harsh reality. A depressing reality. But Sharon, like so many other caring individuals, refuses to let her spirits be crushed.

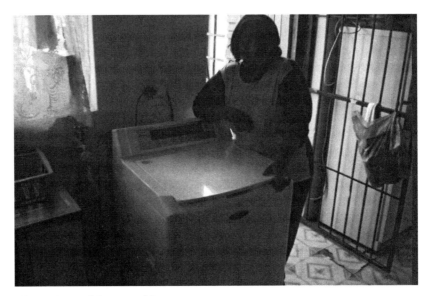

Sharon's washing machine

One month after I met Sharon, a washing machine was installed and paid for by HOPE. A washing machine will not stop the spread of AIDS, or prevent hunger, but for Sharon it makes a difference to her everyday life. So many children depend on her. The washing machine conserves her personal energy and gives her more time to be with the children that need her most. We have also funded vital roof repairs to the crèche. Sharon could never find the money to repair her roof, but thanks to HOPE, she can now get on with the job of repairing the broken hearts of her orphans. That's money very well spent. Our South African representative, Elisabeth Anderson, has reported back on Sharon's crèche and other projects in the Cape Town area and has continued to keep the wheels of HOPE turning. She has given her time and energy to our projects in South Africa. I would like to acknowledge her retirement in 2007 and the amount of wonderful work she did for HOPE in Cape Town and beyond.

In the North of South Africa, hundreds of miles away from Cape Town, in the rural village of Mashau, HOPE has paid for a much needed water supply for a local primary school.

The money for this project was made available from one of our supporters, Liz Baxendale. Liz was a headmistress of a local school. She was a great teacher and she believed in the importance of education. When she died, her family made a decision that instead of friends and family buying flowers for her funeral, that they would make a contribution to HOPE. Good decision. Her money was soon going to make a difference to so many lives. A plaque was made in her memory and presented to the school. "We thank you," the children echoed. They meant every word.

Children of Mashau School receive the Liz Baxendale plaque from Julia Childs

The water supply was drilled in May 2007. It was a great day for the village. That precious supply has helped provide a vital slice of education for the children. As well as being taught to read and write, the pupils of Mashau primary school, under the guidance of an inspirational principal Dr Thamba Rabothata, are taught how to plant, cultivate and of course water their own food. It's a crucial lesson for the future of every one of the children. If they know the fundamentals of farming, they will survive. If their future is not prosperous they will be able to grow their own food. They will not go hungry.

Behind the school, a large plot of land is given over for this valuable lesson. Carrots, aubergines, spinach, potatoes and onions are being tended by the children. The water supply is vital for the harvest. And what a harvest they reap. Fantastic, organic vegetables are pulled from the earth and cooked up at lunchtime for those in need. For some of the youngsters, it is the only meal of the day. When school breaks up at Easter and Christmas, they often go hungry. The whole village supports the agricultural school project. Parents come and help with the allotment. They dig, till the land, water the soil and watch the food grow. Without water, it cannot survive. Surplus vegetables are sold. The money goes back into the school. Liz would be satisfied that her money has been very well spent. Her name lives on in a small village in South Africa.

I sometimes wish all our supporters could visit a HOPE project just once in their lifetime. To walk with the children, see the smiles and witness where our funds are spent is a great lesson in life. We do make a difference to so many of those who may have given up hope.

Children with their new teddies

Every time I visit South Africa, I always take time to step inside the high walled, high security Pollsmoor Prison. It's not a place for the faint hearted. Hardened murderers are locked up within its walls. HIV spreads rapidly amongst the inmates. Rape and bullying is part of the daily life. There are 5,000 adult males in Pollsmoor, 2,000 juveniles as well as more than 400 women inmates, twenty of them with babies.

Amongst the prison population are numerous young, frightened inmates who are still awaiting trial. Some of them have been there for more than a year. Some of them may be innocent, but they remain imprisoned until their trial reaches the courts.

Inmates are only allowed one hour outside their cells. They are in desperate need of physical activity. One important programme in the prison has been set up by Ambassadors In Sport (AIS), a Christian based organisation that has introduced football to the prison. They have made a huge impact in the prison and have recently set up a Soccer Academy for boys discharged from custody that show particular talent. Through the UK organisation KitAid, I took forty kilos of shorts, shirts and footballs for the Pollsmoor prisoners' football teams. Football means everything in South Africa, especially when you are locked up for the majority of the day. For those prisoners, the kit was worth its weight in gold. I met inmates I had seen the year before. They had not been forgotten. They appreciated the gift.

Flying home from South Africa, I felt totally exhausted, but 100% satisfied that HOPE was making a difference. I am committed to every one of those projects in South Africa and every one of our projects around the world. They all need our support. I cannot turn my back on any of them. I have to find a way to keep them funded. Every time I visit a project it reinforces in my mind just how much those children need HOPE. My 'Make Poverty History' wristband worn daily since 2005 and trips to G8 and 365 Faslane rallys are a constant reminder of the needs and problems of the world.

On the verge of sleep, I often spare a thought for those individuals and children who are in dire need. The faces of

Chapter 27

children I have met and helped often flash through my mind. I have to keep going for their sake. Every day I continue to plough through endless emails, or make and attend appointments and answer phone calls. Retirement is still not an option. But I have cut down on my workload. I only chalk up an average fifty hours work each week now.

28

HOPE Projects

HOPE works in eleven main countries – Sri Lanka, South Africa, Philippines, India, Ghana, Bulgaria, Zimbabwe, Zambia, Uganda, Kenya and the UK. Many more pages of this book could be filled with touching stories about HOPE's numerous projects around the globe. Instead, in their own words, some of the children HOPE has helped and healed, tell their own tales of hope.

Sachita (India)

I am 11 years old. I have two younger sisters. We used to live on the streets of Bangalore in India begging for money. Sometimes, if we did not get enough, we would go hungry and I wanted to cry but I tried to be brave and look after my sisters. Often we did not feel safe and we would run away from bad people. For the past year, thanks to HOPE, our lives have got much better. We now live at a refuge supported by the charity. The people at the refuge are our family. Every night when I go to sleep I feel safe. We don't go hungry and we are going to school for the first time in our lives and learning how to knit and sew. I don't feel lonely anymore. I feel lucky.

Chapter 28

Begging from car drivers

Pradeep (Sri Lanka)

I am Pradeep and I live in Sri Lanka. I have a horrible scar on my tummy because when I was playing with my brother a hidden landmine blew up. I lost my leg. I was so frightened. The hospital managed to save my life and then fitted me with an artificial leg. I am thankful to HOPE because they paid for my treatment, my meals and travel costs to visit a special centre in Colombo where they help me cope without a leg. As I grow I will need a different leg. HOPE will continue to support me. I don't feel sad because I can walk again and play with my friends.

A Sri Lankan amputee

Bintu (Ghana)

I am the youngest of four children living in Ghana. My grandma looks after us all because my parents died of AIDS. My grandma works very hard but she keeps smiling. "Why are you always smiling?" I ask her. She says it's because for the first time in her life she has been able to earn money. HOPE gave our community a small grant to buy materials to make and paint clay pots. Grandma makes lovely pots and sells them at the market. I help her. Now we have a little money I can afford to go to school.

Richard (Zimbabwe)

I feel very proud that I have just taken my final year exams. My ambition is to go to university and become a social worker and then I can help boys like myself that have had a very bad start in life. Two years ago I was very sick and hungry. I was living with my brother on the streets. We were invited to a drop-in centre supported by HOPE. At the centre they fed us and made me better and encouraged me to study. The other children think I am clever but I am just determined to show others that you can lift yourself up in life. HOPE gave me that chance. I try not to look back; instead I look forward to the day when I can go to university.

An African Boy by my grand daughter Sarah Ming, aged 9

Chapter 28

Pavel (Bulgaria)

I am 12 and I live in a children's home in Bulgaria. It used to be very, very cold in the home and in the winter I shivered because we didn't have any heating and my bed only had one thin blanket. Last Christmas was the best ever because HOPE paid for a heating system to be installed and they gave us new blankets and clothes and knitted teddies. My teddy sleeps with me in my warm bed. I feel better now I'm warmer. So does my teddy.

There are many more inspirational stories like these. Sadly, there are also countless other forgotten children in the world that need hope in their lives. The world continues to be a war torn place where poverty brings suffering. The victims are the children. Our mission is to improve the quality of life and advance the rights of all children.

29

Dear Dad

"In your last moments of life, will you be able to say that the world has been a better place because of your presence?"

So what do you think dad? You were the one who asked me that question. You were the one who set me the challenge on the last chapter of your life. If you've been watching over me, if you've seen how my life has unfolded since you died, you will be able to judge for yourself whether 'the world is a better place because of my presence'. I like to think so. I like to think that I have been responsible for shaping the world in some small but significant way.

I hope this airing of my life shows who I am, how I think and what is important to me. I hope it reflects on my contribution to the world and my family. And I hope dad, that if we were granted an hour on this earth together that you would shake my hand, pat me on the back, buy me a pint and be pleasantly surprised at what I've achieved.

30

Favourite Quotes

I have unsuccessfully attempted to find the source of all quotes used. I acknowledge those authors known.

"Some people make it happen, others watch it happen, and some say 'what happened?'"

"The world isn't bad because of all the evil people within it, but because of all the good ones doing nothing."

"Non sibi sed omnibus" – not for oneself, but for others.

"What goes around, comes around."

"There's none so quaint as folk."

"In formation, geese from behind honk to encourage those in front."

"The world holds enough for everyone's need but not for everyone's greed." **Mahatma Gandhi**

"I am convinced that for practical as well as moral reasons, non-violence offers the only road to freedom for my people." **Martin Luther King Jr**

"We praise our soldiers going to war, but forget them when they come back injured." **Rudyard Kipling**

"We have chosen the way of non-violence simply because we think it's politically better for the country in the long run to establish that you can bring about change without the use of arms." **Aung San Suu Kyi**

"To laugh often and much, to win the respect of intelligent people and the affection of children; to earn the appreciation of ones critics and endure the betrayal of false friends; to appreciate beauty, to find the best in others; to leave the world a bit better, whether by a healthy child, a garden patch, or a redeemed social condition; to know that even one life has breathed easier because you have lived. This is to have succeeded." **Emerson**

"Am I bovered? Am I bovered?" **Catherine Tate**

"We all warm ourselves by fires we did not build and drink from wells we did not dig." **Book of Deuteronomy**

Here are a few of my favourite things

Good health
Clearing my desk
Sleep
Meditation and Prayer
Visiting Scotland
Seeing my grand children develop
Walking and swimming
Kippers
Chelsea and Surrey winning
Empathy
Optimism
Humour
Love
Walking the walk
HOPE's continued success

Chapter 30

SHUTTERED MINDS

We close our minds to unending words
Of news and views
Of inhumanity and genocide.

We cannot remember
The incessant chatter
Of the word-processing of constant information.

We see an avalanche
Of TV scenes
Of destruction,
War and brutality.

We meet someone
Who has been a witness
And seen the poverty and brutality
Of distant lives.

So our shuttered minds open
And allow some light and warmth
Into our hearts.

**This poem was specially written for me
by a Quaker friend, Anne Smith.**

Hope for Children (HOPE)

HOPE is about improving the quality of life and advancing the rights of children, specifically assisting children who suffer through being Handicapped, Orphaned, Poor and Exploited.

HOPE carries out much of its work in ten main developing countries – India, Sri Lanka, Philippines, South Africa, Kenya, Zimbabwe, Ghana, Uganda, Zambia and Bulgaria as well as supporting children in the UK. In addition, small annual grants are made to projects in another twenty countries.

HOPE is a small low-cost, 'no frills' charity supporting projects and minimizing administrative and promotional costs through being mainly reliant on voluntary effort.

HOPE supports small, local projects, filling the gaps left by the bigger charities.

HOPE stays in areas where there are continuing needs, when the media and other charities move on.

HOPE works through local Representatives so that project recommendations are determined in country through an annual budget.

HOPE has the support of high profile celebrities including Gary Lineker, Lulu and Justin Rose.

HOPE was registered in the UK in 1994 No:1041258.

YOUR SMALL CHANGE CAN MAKE A BIG CHANGE

Please send any donations to: Hope for Children, HOPE House, 14a Queensway, Hemel Hempstead, Hertfordshire, HP1 1LR. UK.

Tel: 0844 7799774 Fax: 0845 0099628
email: hope@hope4c.org
website: www.hope-for-children.org

Lightning Source UK Ltd.
Milton Keynes UK
02 December 2010

163737UK00004B/1/P